Perfect Phrases for Business School Acceptance

Perfect Phrases for Business School Acceptance

Hundreds of Ready-to-Use Phrases to Write the Attention-Grabbing Essay, Stand out in an Interview, and Gain a Competitive Edge

Paul Bodine

New York Chicago San Francisco Lisbon London
Madrid Mexico City Milan New Delhi San Juan
Seoul Singapore Sydney Toronto

1 2 3 4 5 6 7 8 9 0   DOC/DOC   0 1 4 3 2 1 0 9 8

ISBN   978-0-07-159820-0
MHID   0-07-159820-0

This book is printed on acid-free paper.

McGraw-Hill books are available at special quantity discounts for use as premiums and sales promotions, or for use in corporate training programs. For more information, please write to the Director of Special Sales, McGraw-Hill Professional, Two Penn Plaza, New York, NY, 10121-2298. Or contact your local bookstore.

This publication is designed to provide accurate and authoritative information in regard to the subject matter covered. It is sold with the understanding that neither the author nor the publisher is engaged in rendering legal, accounting, or other professional services. If legal advice or other expert assistance is required, the services of a competent professional person should be sought.

> —*From a Declaration of Principles jointly adopted*
> *By a Committee of the American Bar*
> *Association and a Committee of Publishers.*

Library of Congress Cataloging-in-Publication Data

Bodine, Paul, 1959-
   Perfect phrases for business school acceptance: hundreds of ready-to-use phrases to write the attention-grabbing essay, stand out in an interview, and gain a competitive edge / Paul Bodine.
      p. cm.
   Includes bibliographical references and index.
   ISBN-13: 978-0-07-159820-0 (alk. paper)
   ISBN-10: 0-07-159820-0 (alk. paper)
1. Business schools—United States—Admission. 2. College applications—United States. 3. Essay—Authorship. 4. Exposition (Rhetoric) 5. Business writing. I. Title.
   HF1131.B545 2008
   650.71'173—dc22   2008020243

For my mother, Patricia

Contents

Contents

Chapter 3. Perfect Phrases for Accomplishment Essays   61

Chapter 4. Perfect Phrases for Leadership and Teamwork Essays   83

Part III. Personal Topics   105

Chapter 5. Perfect Phrases for Self-Revelation Essays   107

Contents

Part IV. Other Topics   151

Contents

Chapter 9. Perfect Phrases for Social Impact and Change Essays   193

Part V. Optional Essays and Admissions Interviews   211

Chapter 10. Perfect Phrases for Optional Essays   213

Contents

Chapter 11. Perfect Phrases for Business School Interviews   227

Preface

The MBA is a powerful, versatile, well-remunerated degree—and an increasingly popular one. Today the world's most selective business schools know they'll receive enough applications with outstanding "numbers" (grades and GMATs) and career trajectories to populate multiple entering classes over and over. They can therefore afford to select not only the most capable and impressive class, but also one whose sheer variety and distinctiveness will multiply the learning and insight that take place in the classroom.

To winnow down these vast applicant pools, business schools by necessity look to more subjective selection criteria. The admissions essay and interview enable the admissions committees to look beyond the application data and see the person behind them, to get a sense not only of what the applicant has done but why he or she has done it.

In my over 10 years of admissions consulting experience, I have helped hundreds of applicants gain admission to the most selective business schools in the world, among them Harvard, Stanford, and Wharton, of course, but also the dozens of business schools with less hallowed brands but with comparably outstanding strengths. They all use the admissions essay and interview to see the real person behind the transcripts, score reports, and résumé bullets.

Preface

Writing is hard. Writing essays for business school admission is even harder. This book's "perfect phrases" are intended to help you overcome the paralysis the blank PC screen sometimes inspires by providing sample wording you can use to bridge the gap between outline and first draft. Because generic writing is bad writing, you'll find that the phrases and examples included here are not "one-size-fits all" templates. They contain the concrete details—facts, names, places, numbers—that good writing always has. Use these perfect phrases as prompts, guides, even temporary "crutches" as you work toward a final draft expressed in your own words. But when you reach the point where you're confident in the substance of your essays—when writer's block is no longer an issue—search for ways to turn the perfect phrases you've used into your own words. Your writing and your odds of admission will both benefit.

Letting these perfect phrases become a substitute for your own words defeats the purpose of this book. More importantly, it defeats the purpose of the admissions essay. Business schools don't admit applicants who sound like other applicants or write what they think the schools want to hear. They admit real people who tell their own stories in their own way. Use these perfect phrases to help you do that and only that. Then your essays' phrases will truly be "perfect."

This book focuses on the basic business school essay and interview topic categories. Part I guides you through the sometimes stressful process of writing admissions essays, from selecting your themes, developing your raw material, and preparing an initial outline to writing, revising, and editing your drafts.

Preface

Part II provides dozens of perfect phrases for the core B-school essay topics: goals, accomplishments, and leadership/teamwork. In Part III, we move on to the personal essay topics that virtually every school requires: self-revelation, diversity/cross-cultural, and contribution essays. Part IV provides perfect phrases for essay topics that, while common, are not necessarily found in every business school's essay set: challenge/defining-moment essays, failure and ethics-related essays, and social impact and change/innovation essays. In Part V, you'll find perfect phrases for the ubiquitous optional essay and the ever-important admissions interview.

I welcome any suggestions you have for improving this book; e-mail me at paulbodine@live.com.

Acknowledgments

My thanks to Anya Kozorez of McGraw-Hill for her role in bringing this book about and to my wife, Tamami, for her patience and support during this book's gestation.

Perfect Phrases for Business School Acceptance

Part I

Getting Started

Chapter 1 Writing Business School Essays

The quality and number of applicants competing for the world's most selective business schools climb each year. As they do, the humble admissions essay becomes increasingly decisive in helping MBA programs choose the applicants who will be admitted from the also-rans. This is fortunate for you because the application essay is one of the components of your applications over which you have the greatest control. From the themes you choose to encompass your "profile" and the stories you pick to illustrate them, to the lessons you draw and the tone you adopt, business schools give you the reins to shape how they will perceive your candidacy.

Your Profile and Themes

Before you begin writing your essays, and even before you know the questions your schools ask, you must first develop a short self-marketing message or "profile" that integrates the key themes (strengths, experiences, interests) you want your application to communicate. Take your time in this process. Cast your net widely, and ask friends and family for their input. You want the handful of themes that sum up your profile to reflect the key uniqueness factors that distinguish your professional, personal, community, and academic lives from others.

As a rule of thumb, construct your application's self-marketing profile out of four or five themes, each one rich enough to build an essay around. Ideally, these four or five themes will inform all your essays for every school (albeit with some tweaking here and there to match particular schools' emphases).

Data Mining Your Life

Once you have nailed down your themes, you need to identify the individual stories that you'll build each essay around. You can do this by "data mining" your experiences through résumé-based brainstorming or techniques like daily journaling or stream-of-consciousness writing (aka the "brain dump"). Since your view of your own life is unlikely to be objective, ask friends, family members, and mentors what they think your key traits and accomplishments are.

Performing this life inventory should flush out the stories that best capture your self-marketing themes. However, you also want to be continually asking yourself which stories have the most value or significance. A story's external significance could include its impact on your career progress (promotions, raises, career switches), your organization (landing a new client, developing a new product), or others (helping a teen earn A's). A story's internal significance would include how the experience changed you, enhanced your skills, deepened your perspective, strengthened your sense of your potential, and so on.

If you've done it right, your data-mining process should leave you with a mass of raw material that could fill dozens of admissions essays. Because you approached the data-mining stage with your four or five themes already defined, however, you should be able to group your raw stories or data points into buckets that correspond to those themes.

Now you should begin to evaluate your raw stories critically. Look for experiences that capture in microcosm what's essential about you so you'll avoid "overview" essays that only skim many key moments. Ideally, you'll find stories that capture all four or five of the themes in your profile. By understanding these stories, someone can know as much about who you really are as by hearing your full autobiography. Look for the stories that are most distinctive and that combine the greatest external impact and personal transformation. If a story is rating high in distinctiveness, objective results or impact, and personal significance, you've probably got a keeper. Subject all the raw stories generated by your data-mining process to this same weighing or ranking process until you've arrived at a core set of stories that covers all the topics for the application you plan to tackle first.

Essay Topics

Your next step is to connect your stories to schools' specific essay topics. But which topics? Most business schools' essays come down to these eight basic subject areas:

- Goals (including "why an MBA" and "why our school").
- Accomplishments or impact stories.

- Leadership and teamwork experiences.
- Self-revelation topics (including autobiographical, values, and hobbies/passions essays).
- Diversity and cross-cultural essays and your potential contribution to your classmates.
- Failure or setback experiences.
- Ethics-related stories.
- Social impact and change/innovation topics.

This book provides perfect phrases for all these topics. Study carefully the wording of each question in your target school's essay set to determine which of these topics may be lurking there. Schools put a great deal of thought into their essay topics because they're looking for the wording that will get you to open up and show them who you are and what drives you. Unfortunately, you won't usually be able to simply match each of your four or five themes to each school's essay questions, one to one. Some schools may force you to discuss several of your themes in a single essay. Other schools may pose questions that none of your self-marketing themes seem appropriate for. Many essay questions ask you to address several things, so pay special attention both to the question's subject words (for example, "career progress" and "nonprofessional accomplishment") as well as the direction words ("describe," "discuss," "explain"). Read carefully, break out all the subquestions, and even e-mail the school for clarification if you need to, but be sure you know what you're being asked.

Now you're ready to start the essays themselves.

Writing Your Essays

An outline is a useful device for reducing the anxiety and the time drain of the writing process. By bringing structure to your essay before you start writing it, outlines maximize your efficiency and enable you to perform a crucial early test of your essay ideas before you've invested too much in them. The outlines you prepare for business school admissions essays will have their own distinctive structure, usually some variation of the following:

- Introduction
- Context
- What you did
- Result
- Takeaways

The introduction is the initial wording that establishes the essay's tone and tries to get the reader interested in the story you're about to tell. The context section states the challenge, problem, or situation that required you to act.

The "what you did" section is the heart of the essay—a concrete description of the steps or actions you took to address the challenge, resolve the problem, or change the situation you presented in your context section. It will live or die by the degree of personal, vivid detail, and insight you provide. You want to achieve a balance between "data"—the facts that substantiate your themes—and "analysis"—that is, regularly stepping back from an example or anecdote to tell the reader what it means.

Your essay's result section concretely states the outcome or impact of your actions—what was the "end state" after you did what you did? The takeaways section explains what you learned from the experience, and the conclusion is the closing wording that creates a sense of "summing up," often by referring back in some way to the introduction but with a forward-looking twist.

This five-part structure is not intended as a one-size-fits-all formula. Sometimes an essay's introduction can include a description of the context, for example, just as the conclusion and the takeaways can be combined. And as we'll see, goals essays are organized in a very different way. But for most business school admissions essays, this structure can reliably guide you as you decide how best to tell your stories. In fact, the perfect phrases in this book have been organized wherever possible into these basic essay components.

First Drafts

Your focus when writing the first draft of your essay is really just to get something down on paper. Many applicants believe they have to complete a polished, finished draft in the first sitting. The result is usually a starchy, formal-sounding treatise without life or detail. Don't be so hard on yourself! Good writing is a base-at-a-time game; it's not about home runs. Forget about style, grammar, and word count when writing your first draft. It's been said that writing a first draft should take no more than 15 percent of your total essay-writing time. So, relax, run with your outline, and don't overanalyze what you're writing—just get it down.

Writing Business School Essays

To overcome the anxiety of the blank screen and the feeling that admissions essays are a task or chore, try the following experiment. Think of your essays not as arguments ("Why I should be admitted") or proposals ("Admit me for the following reasons"), but as stories about an interesting and sympathetic hero—you—in pursuit of a distant but holy grail: the MBA. People are hardwired to respond to such human-interest stories. We like happy endings. Tales of sympathetic protagonists overcoming conflict or obstacles by changing their environments to remove those conflicts or obstacles appeal to our basic hopes. Impersonal proposals do not. Many applicants' essays sound identical, and the reason for this is almost always a lack of specific human detail and personal anecdotes. So as you're writing your essay, always be as personal and specific as you can.

Revising

Once you have written a rough draft based on your outline, step back and consider macro and organizational changes, such as contradictory themes or assertions, needlessly repeated points, gaps in context or logic, or weakly developed or poorly placed paragraphs. Continually ask yourself whether your main thesis and secondary points will be clear to the admissions readers, whether your evidence will persuade them, whether you are telling this story as efficiently and clearly as you can. Have you included enough material to support your assertions or illustrate your experiences? Does the lesson you're trying to draw from your material have enough substance or does it seem superficial or clichéd? Does it really grow organically from the story itself, or does it seem imposed and unearned?

If you find any of these issues (and you probably will), you may need to switch around paragraphs, cut digressions, or add to, delete, or bolster your examples. But don't get stressed out. Remember, you already have your structure and rough draft, so it's basically all downhill from here. Depending on how good your outline is and how well you fleshed it out in your first draft, your essay may go through one, two, or even more macro-level revisions before it's ready for editing proper.

Editing

The next stage, editing, means cleaning up the essay's mechanics and grammar at the sentence and word level. The potential glitches that editing catches can be everything from pronoun and subject-verb agreement, dangling modifiers, run-on sentences, and parallelism to punctuation and capitalization errors, word choice and misspelling, and active- versus passive-voice issues. One overriding rule that should guide your editing: Always choose the simplest, shortest, and most direct expression over the more complex or seemingly sophisticated one. Read your essays aloud. Do they flow? Is the tone conversational, and does it sound like you?

Your essay is finished when you can't imagine how to make it say what you mean more candidly, vividly, or directly. When you've achieved that level of honesty, color, and tautness, let go.

Part II

Core Topics: Goals, Accomplishments, and Leadership

Chapter 2 Perfect Phrases for Goals Essays

"Describe your career progress to date and your future short-term and long-term career goals. How do you expect a Wharton MBA to help you achieve these goals, and why is now the best time for you to join our program?"

(Wharton)

"Why are you pursuing an MBA at this point in your career? Describe your personal and professional goals and the role an MBA from the University of Chicago GSB plays in your plans to reach these goals."

(Chicago)

The goals essay is the single most important essay that business schools require because it's where you answer the question that justifies your entire application: why do you need an MBA? But as the two sample questions above indicate, goals essays rarely ask just this question. They also want you to state your post-MBA goals and to connect those goals with your career path. And that's not all. Most schools also want to know not only why you want an MBA, but why an MBA from their program. Then there's the "why now?" question. Some schools ask it explicitly, but even when they don't, you should address it.

Because of the goals essay's importance (it's probably the one essay topic that *every* business school requires), this chapter contains the largest number of perfect phrases. Fortunately, we've divided them into the rough order in which you'll normally use them in the essay:

- Introductions
- Career progress
- Goals
- Why an MBA?
- Why an MBA now?
- Why our school?
- Conclusions

Introductions

Because the goals essay forces you to cover so much ground, it's often not the best place to try out your most "creative" writing ideas. But this doesn't mean that you need to start the essay with, "I need an MBA to become an investment banker." A well-conceived introduction can inspire the admissions staff's interest in you from the very start. We've divided the following introduction phrases into six categories, but they by no means exhaust the options available to you.

To-the-Point Introductions

- Fourteen years is a long time in any industry. In consumer software, it's an eternity.
- My fascination with the human resources function began in college.
- Is there such a thing as an entrepreneurial gene?
- I am a Botswanan who is optimistic about Botswana.
- My current position—project manager at PeopleCare Health Sciences—is the direct result of three key decisions.
- Five years ago, the meaning of the acronym "MBA" was completely unknown to me.
- I aspire to build a company that develops cutting-edge food industry technology better, faster, and cheaper than any other company around today.
- My job as a naval flight officer has taken me all over the world.
- What is an animal rights activist doing applying to business school?
- As the child of two doctors, a fascination with the secrets of life science was my birthright.

- At ExxonMobil we are coping with fundamental trends in the oil industry that threaten the very nature of our business.

Quotations as Introductions

- "We are drowning in information, but starving for knowledge." John Naisbett's words describe in a nutshell what I regard as the central challenge facing the demand forecasting business.

- "Look at how many people believe in us." Grinning proudly, Bruce Okura, SeedBank's CEO, passed around the largest check I'd ever seen—for $8 million.

- "There will never be a big company in that region." The source of that disparaging take on my home country's prospects was none other than a senior investment banking group manager at Morgan Stanley, New York. If anyone should know whether East Africa could sustain a major industrial enterprise it would be him. And yet, as I heard his words, I knew with conviction that he was wrong.

- "… Estoy sorprendido pero feliz y creo que estás una muy buena gerente de consultoría." Those were the musical words that Pablo Suarez, my Denso Mexico manager, used in introducing my first performance review.

- "You are Sid Taneyev, right?" To a junior technical staffer less than a year out of grad school, hearing those five friendly words from OrbProcom's CEO seemed about as likely as being told Bill Gates was holding for me on line two.

- "Money has no ideas. Only ideas make money"— J. Séguéla

Scene-setting Introductions

- It's an early Monday morning in January 2007, and across the conference table from me sits Boonklee Shinawatra, the CFO of Siam Central Holdings, the largest industrial company in Thailand. I have just finished presenting the project financing my crack nine-member team has crafted to fund the launch of Siam Central's Bangkok Diamond Palace, the largest luxury resort and gaming center in Southeast Asia. To say the least, I am excited at the prospect of closing this $1.9 billion transaction.

- "Ladies and gentlemen, we are approaching Bishkek, the capital city of Kyrgyzstan. We thank you for flying Kyrgyzstan Air." With the pilot's announcement, I knew that the 12-hour return flight from London to my homeland was almost over. It was my first trip home since I had left for the United Kingdom five years before, a scared, nervous, and excited 20-year-old. Returning to Bishkek for summer holiday, I was about to introduce my wife Beatrice to 16 family members who weren't able to attend our wedding two years before.

- The fresh smell of tortillas fill the air as the farmers' kids swing their sticks at the swaying piñata. The adults of Bello Campo all huddle together to discuss the upcoming workweek and boast about their kids' accomplishments in school. As the dust settles and the sun sets, the families say their good-byes and slowly retreat to their homes. A typical birthday party in the small town of Huauchinango, Mexico, draws to a close.

- Sounds from a folk festival in La Gombe Central Park follow me as I walk back to my new Kinshasa home. It is November 27, 2007, and thousands are singing and dancing in celebration of the first anniversary of Joseph Kabila's free election as president of the Democratic Republic of Congo. Only five years had passed since my sister stunned me with the news that Kabila's father, Laurent, had been assassinated by his bodyguard. In that moment, my career and my life suddenly changed.

- Then, cresting the waves south of New Zealand, Subodh and I suddenly came upon a massive, steel-gray whaling ship—a "sushi factory on steroids," he called it—anchored stolidly in the icy waters. "That's the *Otaru Maru*," Subodh exclaimed with a mixture of fear and disgust.

Attention-Grabbing Introductions

- On April 2, 2004, a sightseeing plane that was giving me and four college friends a bird's-eye tour of the Virgin

Islands plunged into the Atlantic Ocean after the left engine caught fire. By the time I reached the door, the plane was already submerged.

- I am a citizen of an invisible country. For too many years, Burma, the largest country in southeast Asia—now called "Myanmar" by its military dictators—has been ignored by the world.

- Fifteen thousand people, 100,000 sheep, no traffic lights. The bare figures never do justice to my hometown in New Zealand.

- I must be crazy. To my classmates, a complete loss of reason was the only possible explanation for my decision to walk away from the success guaranteed by an elite French business degree for the unknown.

- Who are these strange-looking people in my living room?

- I'm a girdle engineer. That's what I tell people. Though it always gets a laugh or smile, girdles—for men and for women—along with our other consumer products are definitely big business.

- Setting diamonds isn't the usual entry to financial services, I'll admit.

Industry-Focused Introductions

- When I think of Japanese companies, Sony comes to mind. When I think of American companies, I picture

Google, Microsoft, and GE. When I think of New Zealand companies, however, no firm that is globally recognized as a successful enterprise comes to mind.

- Today, there are more than 1,500 biotechnology firms in North America; only 50 of them are profitable.

- In 2007, Uruguay completed its fourth consecutive year of 6 percent or higher economic growth. U.S. imports from Uruguay ballooned to over $650 million.

- With 530,000 flights, 100 million passengers, and 7 million tons of cargo annually, the Dubai International Airport is expected to be one of the world's largest airports by 2020.

- The infrastructure of the United States is close to the breaking point. Sixty-four thousand railroad bridges need upgrading, 4 million utility poles must be replaced annually, 1.8 million highway sign posts need repair.

- India's business process outsourcing industry is exploding. According to the McKinsey-NASSCOM 2005 report, India's BPO sector will grow from $11.6 billion in 2006 to $150 billion by 2010.

Autobiographical Introductions

- Twenty years ago, I was herding goats and driving cattle-driven carriages through the small village of Senerhat, Bangladesh. Today, I use state-of-the-art animation software to perform complex visualizations in designing the world's most realistic videogaming products.

- When I was a kid, I wanted to be a cab driver.
  I considered it a challenging profession that required the rare ability to gauge traffic movements throughout the city, instinctively calculate possible routes, and anticipate your next moves to find the quickest path to your destination. Today I manage $560 million in invested assets.

- The steam locomotive ride from my hometown of Kluchi, Kamchatka, to Milkovo, where I went to high school, was both a social affair and a lesson in life.

Career Progress

The purpose of the career progress section is basically to get you to account for where your post-MBA goals come from. What experiences and interests have shaped your career objectives? You should also use this section to explain the key decision or inflection points in your career and to briefly communicate what's impressive or atypical about it. If space permits, you can even work in a mini-accomplishment or two as well.

- Everything I have done professionally is focused on this entrepreneurial goal. After joining Altria South America, I was promoted annually until I reached market manager in only three years—a position usually granted only after five years. Now I am responsible for sales in South America's biggest market, contributing approximately $120 million in annual revenue, or 3 percent of our revenues. For the past three years, I have consistently been rated one of the top two performers among all 30 market managers at Altria South America.

- Within eighteen months of joining Lenovo's R&D lab in Hong Kong, I had been promoted twice, from eBusiness analyst to R&D project manager and then R&D product manager. At the same time, my R&D budget grew from $290,000 in 2003 to $1.5 million by the end of 2005. After initially managing one person on one R&D project in 2003, I now manage seven different R&D projects involving 15 full-time employees and seven consultants representing nine different nationalities. At least 75 percent of my work time now involves managing the work of others, most of whom are at least 10 years older than me.

- While these launch projects introduced me to entrepreneurship and enabled me to focus on strategic-level business issues, they lacked the corporate social responsibility focus I had enjoyed in my work at Deutsche Telekom. In August 2007, I therefore joined Dreams Alive, an Angolan micro finance nongovernmental organization (NGO), where as a product manager I help launch and expand microenterprises by introducing nonfinancial products and services such as business training.

■ I have earned a level of responsibility that it normally takes trained aviation industry professionals five years to achieve. My rapid success has brought me to the point where it's prudent to take stock and ask myself where I want the rest of my career to go. If I stay in aviation much longer, I may pigeonhole myself, a fate it's not so easy to escape.

■ Venture capital has been an exciting change. By focusing on start-up companies like OnJoy, Flickable Technologies, and DazzleSoft in two different industries—wireless networks and integrated development environments—I have gained experience in management and investment analysis, enterprise coaching and mentoring, and management recruiting.

■ Eight months ago, Metrics Vision engaged Boston Consulting Group to help us refine our business strategy in the market research space. I provided the BCG consultants with the information and resources they needed to make their recommendations. Since I had primarily done technical consulting at Inforte, BCG's strategy-focused consulting was new and extremely exciting to me. In talking with the BCG consultants, I discovered that strategy work requires not only great "vision," analytical ability, and leadership skills but also a solid understanding of business decision making, fundamentals, and corporate strategy.

- Deciding to make the shift into private equity, I joined Sun Capital Partners. This change brought me closer to the management dynamics of real companies and exposed me to more functions of business, which will clearly benefit me when I become an entrepreneur. As a private equity manager, I confront the same issues, whether legal, strategic, or operational, that companies' CEOs grapple with.

- I enjoyed great experiences and success at Ingram Micro: a rare double promotion in 2005, several salary increases, and the coveted opportunity to write an internal white paper. However, in August 2006, just before that year's review process, I made the measured decision to leave for Menglun & Co., a young technology and strategy consultancy. I left to challenge my leadership and managerial skills in a smaller, more entrepreneurial environment where drive, focus, and an opportunistic mindset translated directly and immediately into success.

- I majored in business to get a broad understanding of the fundamentals. After graduating from Western Ontario, I joined Ernst & Young to gain business experience in a variety of industries. In my five years with the firm, I have served clients in banking, health care, and insurance. My exposure to different business situations and problems has sharpened my analytical skills, and through my managerial duties on different projects, I have developed my leadership, management, communication, and interpersonal skills. After five years of solid skill building, however, I believe something is still missing.

- After one and a half years, I was promoted to consultant, an entry level for MBAs, which enabled me to take on more leadership roles by supervising one or two business analysts or associate consultants. And this year, I was promoted to senior consultant even though I still lack an MBA (more than 90 percent of the 250 consultants at New Haven Associates hold either an MBA or a Ph.D.). Today, I am proud to be leading 10 to 20 client project team members, coaching new consultants, presenting final reports, and advising clients' senior management.

- I saw how a company of 10,000 employees allocates its resources to make a mainframe computer in two years. Seeing managers orchestrate the work of hundreds of engineers made me want to understand this management process from a higher level. At IBM, I was responsible for the first time for complete projects and for managing outside consulting resources to accomplish our milestones. Planning, budgeting, recruiting, and customer relationships became familiar functions that fit into my more strategic perspective of what makes effective organizations work.

Goals

No need to get fancy here—just state your post-MBA path. But be concrete. Mention likely job titles, probable industry niches, companies you'd like to join, key skills you hope to develop in each role, any regional or geographical preferences. Most of all, specify the evolution of your post-MBA career path over time: short term, intermediate (if relevant), long term.

Short-Term Goals

- As I learned more about finance careers from colleagues, investment banking became my focus. After research in books about the industry and conversations with bankers like Susan Wilson (HSBC) and Nitin Verma (Lehman Brothers), I have focused my goal on becoming an associate in corporate finance at Goldman Sachs or Morgan Stanley, renowned for their comprehensive training programs. Over three or four years as an associate, I will learn how to enhance client relationships, structure and execute financial transactions, work effectively with and learn from high-level executives, and gain broad expertise across products, industries, and regions.

- My short-term career objective is to work in a venture capital company such as Azione Capital or in a direct investment company that invests in emerging markets.

Ideally, I would like to be based in London and to be responsible for managing investments in Eastern Europe or Asia. As an investment manager, I would assess the risk and reward profiles of companies in several different countries, which would require a thorough understanding of both the complex operating environments of those companies and the rapidly changing landscape of the international capital markets. Such a dual role would allow me to leverage the analytical skills and work experience I have gained as a telecom and media analyst in France as well as the solid foundation in finance I will acquire at INSEAD.

- In the near term, a management consulting position with a boutique firm such as Tiburon Strategic Advisors will give me the chance to practice my newfound skills and gain a wider perspective on the financial services industry. By working on multiple turnaround management, project finance, and productivity assignments, in a short time I will benefit from seeing what has and hasn't worked in the real world. I believe consulting represents the best way for me to start out making professional contacts and using the skills I will gain at Haas.

- My short-term goal after earning my MBA is to leverage my Tuck contacts and credentials to move into the investment/asset management industry as an equity research analyst for a Canada-based asset management firm such as CIBC. In addition, I plan to study for the CFA exam at Tuck and pass it shortly after graduating. I will spend the first four to five years of my post-MBA career learning the investment management and mutual fund industries, after which I will manage a relatively smaller equity fund.

- Tajikistan needs Western investment to help drill the oil and managers with financial skills to help promote this investment. That is why my short-term career goal is to become the finance officer of a Western company seeking to invest in Tajikistan, for example, a multinational (such as ExxonMobil or British Petroleum) investing in the Tajikistan-Caspian pipeline. In this stage of my career I will evaluate investment risks, analyze acquisitions, participate in the negotiations for acquisitions, and perform financial planning, capital budgeting, and forecasting.

- My short-term post-MBA objective is to secure a senior management position with the Japanese branch of McKinsey, BCG, or Bain. During this stage of my career, I want to develop wide-angle expertise in directing business operations and managing big-picture strategic plans and, in particular, to acquire broader exposure to corporate issues in the specific macroeconomic environment of Japan and Korea. At the same time, I will firm up my own entrepreneurial business plan; establish business partnerships; raise capital for my future company; and detail my plans for my company's R&D, manufacturing, and marketing.

■ My short-term goals are to develop the skills I will need to run my future start-up by earning an MBA and gaining experience in all the cross-functional areas of business, from marketing to finance. To achieve the latter goal, I will split my MBA internship between two industries. First, by working in business development at SprintNextel or NextWave Wireless, I will learn how to convince companies to participate in the WiMax space. Second, by working in vendor management at a technology manufacturing company such as GE or United Technologies, I will learn how to establish relationships with external manufacturers. For two to three years after graduation, I will broaden my knowledge of and nurture contacts in the technology manufacturing industry while I develop my business plan.

■ My short-term goal is to gain exposure to three or four major business areas by rotating through several divisions of a pharmaceutical company or an established biotech company, such as Biogen Idec or Human Genome Sciences. Specifically, since I already have a solid base in strategy (from my time at McKinsey) and in finance/accounting (through Apax Partners), I would like to spend several years in operations and marketing so I can gain experience running a manufacturing plant and launching a new product. During business school, I would seek out a summer internship with a biotech or pharmaceutical company to give my candidacy more credibility for the post-MBA recruiting phase. When I graduate, I plan to join a larger, established biotech firm where I can acquire the most diverse learning opportunities. For example, Biogen Idec has an MBA training program in sales and marketing that consists of a sales rotation out in the field selling products to oncology or neurological customers or managing strategic corporate accounts. After the first 12 months, the employee joins the marketing team back at headquarters.

- To realize my objectives, my short-term goal is to combine an MBA with my experiences as an auditor and corporate finance analyst so I can gain an associate position in a corporate advisory group of a bulge bracket investment bank like Credit Suisse. By devoting the first stage of my post-MBA career to analyzing mergers, divestitures, and capital market transactions, I can learn how to use modeling techniques to determine the dilution to earnings per share in an all-stock acquisition, compute the stand-alone value of a subsidiary during a divestiture, or calculate the amount of free cash flow a company can generate to cover a new issuance of debt. I will also be able to see firsthand how the management teams I advise and work for handle complex negotiations, high-impact decision making, and volatile scenarios. In short, an associate position will enable me to begin building a best-practices knowledge base of both technical and management skills that I can apply as a senior banker later in my career.

- To achieve this future, my short-term objective is to work as a developer/strategist for a major infrastructure development firm such as Samsung or Hochtief. Since any major development effort in the United Arab Emirates is likely to be spearheaded by these large firms, I want to bring my international experience in project finance to them so I can gain more executive-level experience in project financing and development. A second option I am considering is to join a governmental organization such as the Infrastructure Investment Center of United Arab Emirates (IICUAE), where I would serve as an investment facilitator, decision maker, and strategic planner. In contrast to the role the developer plays in a single project, for IICUAE I would be able to work from a broader perspective, develop a better understanding of macro strategy and urban planning, and ultimately concentrate on developing new investment and development policies and laying the groundwork for projects that will affect our entire society.

- In the short-term, I will become a prominent actor in business development for the biopharmaceutical industry, and in particular the late drug-development, market-approval, and drug-distribution stages. To achieve that goal, after my MBA I want to join the business development department of a biopharmaceutical firm in Silicon Valley, such as SciClone or Neurok Pharma. Thus I will enlarge my competencies from pure biotech R&D to clinical development, drug production, and commercialization. In this position, I will establish development strategies to create value, sign deals and collaborations with other companies, assess acquisition opportunities, and interact with investors. I will therefore need to understand my firm's core technologies in the global market, have deep expertise in the biotech and pharmaceutical industry, master finance, and have outstanding negotiation skills.

- In the short-term I will join a company such as IKEA or Gap that is renowned for its commitment to social responsibility and its design excellence. There I can acquire insight into the intricacies of a global consumer-goods supply chain as well as firsthand knowledge of effective methods for balancing long-term sustainable commerce programs with quarterly earnings targets.

Intermediate Goals

- In the medium term, say four to six years, my goal is to become the director of new product/business development.

■ My intermediate career objective is to transition into a management role for a key multinational client firm such as Taiwan's Hon Hai Precision Industry or Brazil's Embraer, where I would gain exposure to the operational challenges of line management and the specific issues that face emerging-market corporations, while I also build my network.

■ My intermediate post-MBA objective is to sharpen my consulting expertise, refine my e-commerce strategy for serving family-owned business clients, and gain a better perspective on family business consulting. To do that, I will join a management consulting firm, like McKinsey & Co., that has expertise both in serving family business clients and e-commerce. At the same time, I will establish a solid business network with other professional services that are serving family businesses, for example, by attending worldwide conferences held by such organizations as Family Business Institute or Loyola Family Business Center.

Long-Term Goals

■ The opportunity that leads me to Carnegie Mellon is the challenge of introducing a new intermediate-market model for management consulting. I want to establish a consulting firm that focuses on the customers that are too small for the likes of the Bains and BCGs but too big for the small local consulting firms. These medium-sized clients, with annual revenue of between $100 million and $1 billion, represent a large percentage of America's young, growing companies. My firm will be regionally based but with a strategy for branching out after we establish name recognition. Our competitive advantage will derive from better recruiting standards than small consultancies use today and the balance we will strike between an elite strategy firm's culture and the smaller firm's agile infrastructure.

- My long-term career aspiration is to become a senior vice president of international business development for a major global software company, with responsibility for managing its investments and operations all over the world. This position will allow me to create a business that will help provide technological support to the developing countries in the Balkans, a growing region of more than 55 million inhabitants. I want to contribute to shaping this region's development by creating partnerships between Eastern European and Western companies, enabling technology transfers, and running the operations that create jobs there.

- My long-term objective is to help develop Chile's recently deregulated telecom industry by starting a Santiago-based consulting company that assists aspiring Chilean technology entrepreneurs in developing the managerial knowledge to build and sustain their companies. My company will help them identify opportunities, build strategic partnerships and joint ventures, and obtain domestic and foreign funding. We will also advise the Chilean government in defining telecom and technology policies that encourage the development of socially responsible enterprises, for example, by giving companies economic incentives to develop infrastructure in rural and underdeveloped areas (where 80 percent of Chileans live). In doing so, we can have a positive, lasting influence on the economic and social development of our country.

■ My long-term goal is to establish a for-profit business that provides telephone and Internet connectivity for the rural and poverty-stricken population of Bangladesh. My research and my conversations with experts like Dr. Amit Malhotra have revealed that a broad telecom network is the key to catalyzing the entire economic development process in the Indian subcontinent. Widespread telecom service will not only increase the efficiency of people's everyday lives but will also provide a two-way channel for promoting and distributing goods and services. My firm would start by focusing our implementation efforts on the rural areas near major cities like Dhaka and Chittagong; we would then branch out from there. Since poor people cannot individually afford a telephone connection, let alone a computer, we would market the service to communities such as villages, and individual users would make payments every time they used the resource. Although this model is not a unique one, so far it has been implemented only on a small-scale.

- My long-term career plan is to return to a private sector–focused international developmental organization, such as the International Finance Corp., in a more policy-making capacity. In such a position, I would be able to use my years of experience in the private sector as well as my five years' working within the IFC to formulate policies that fuel economic growth in developing countries.

- I will return to Mexico to fulfill my long-term goal— starting up my own biotech venture. My firm's first priority will be to use its advanced gene-therapy approaches to develop drugs that cure diseases that Mexican people are more likely to contract, such as heart disease and diabetes. My firm will emphasize research and development to secure a strong foothold at the high-quality, premium end of Mexico's pharmaceutical industry. Then I will develop strategic partnerships with global pharmaceutical companies such as GlaxoSmithKline and Sanofi-Aventis to expand my business to the U.S. and European markets while helping them increase their market share in Mexico and Central America.

- In the long term, I want to head the business development branch of a start-up company or to market derivative financial products at a boutique investment bank specializing in international markets. I would most likely achieve this latter goal by initially pursuing a position in equity derivatives trading or on a high-yield fixed income desk. Alternatively, I may pursue a position as an associate in either the corporate finance or mergers and acquisitions division at a leading investment bank such as Lehman Brothers or Morgan Stanley.

- My long-term career plans are twofold. My primary objective some six years after graduating from Emory is to advance to a senior-level management position with an investment bank (such as Merrill Lynch or Goldman Sachs) that deals with strategy and international management. My second long-term career goal, some 12 years after earning my MBA, is to establish my own consulting company that focuses on small- to medium-sized multinational companies seeking opportunities to break ground in Morocco.

- Because the 20 South Korean chaebols account for almost 80 percent of the economy, the next logical stop for me is to transfer my management consulting experience into the manufacturing sector by managing the finances and business decisions of a chaebol. For example, I could restructure the debt of a company like

Hyundai Heavy Industries or plan the strategic management of LG Electronics by, for example, reorganizing its appliance and digital display divisions.

- In the longer term, beginning in my early fifties, I will serve for 5 to 10 years as an economics advisor to the Taiwanese government. My financial independence will guarantee the integrity of my decisions, and my extensive business expertise and industry contacts will ensure that my recommendations are effective and enjoy broad support. Finally, in my late fifties I will establish a nonprofit foundation dedicated to educating underprivileged children in a setting that provides them not only with education but a caring family environment.

- I intend to start an Internet-based health-care service in Russia that provides free medical information. Russian consumers often do not have enough basic medical knowledge to feel comfortable asking doctors for information about their conditions. One of the business schemes I am evaluating is to provide this information by charging advertising fees from professional medical service providers and pharmaceutical companies. My firm will raise the quality of Russia's health-care service by leveraging the demographic aging of the Russian population, the expansion of the Internet from urban to rural markets, and the Russian government's efforts to incentivize doctors to offer better health care.

Why an MBA?

Why you need an MBA and why you need one from, say, Harvard Business School are two related but distinct questions. Many schools ask you to address both. Avoid the generic "strengthen my skill set" response and get concrete.

- A challenging MBA program will give me a thorough grounding in the skills of entrepreneurship—locating and winning seed money, developing a business plan, and integrating technology with the marketing, engineering, and financial functions of a start-up firm. It offers me the most rigorous, efficient, and accelerated way to transition into entrepreneurship.

- A graduate management education will give me intensive exposure to all the major business functional areas I need to strengthen in order to further my managerial career, from marketing, strategy, and production to operations and organizational behavior. Without an MBA, it might take me seven to ten years to acquire all these necessary business skills on the job. Moreover, the pace and flexibility of my growth would be limited by the trap developers often face: being pigeonholed as "techies" rather than managers. Finally, besides the general management and entrepreneurial skills an MBA program will give me, in business school I can exchange ideas with peers from every industry, developing a practical network of contacts essential to my ultimate goal of starting my own dental technology business.

- Effective CFOs must possess a richly varied set of business skills. Some of these skills, such as negotiation ability and communications prowess, can be learned outside the classroom. However, I will soon reach the limit of my ability to "self-train" in the skills I need to become a CFO. Some of these skills—finance, statistics, and managerial economics—cannot really be mastered on the job. I can learn them thoroughly and at a greatly accelerated pace in a challenging MBA program.

- I believe successful managers are holistic. Today, when I go to clients and tell them that I can provide solutions to their organizational process issues, they sometimes remain unconvinced by my experience because my engineering degree creates the impression that I am unqualified to make strategic-level recommendations. It often takes a lot of convincing to get assigned these nontechnical responsibilities, and I have lost great opportunities because I did not have the instant value recognition that a widely respected business degree confers. My managers have assured me that an MBA will accelerate my path to strategy manager, where I can lead the programs we are now bidding on.

- By serving as a technical liaison between sales, engineering, manufacturing, and production at Toyota for five years, I developed unusually rich cross-functional and multitasking skills. These general skills will translate directly into the marketing environment, but I need an MBA to help me fill in my knowledge gaps. For instance, I would like to better understand the principles of advertising and promotion and learn to interpret statistical data from external customers. I am also very interested in how product pricing, strategic planning, and joint ventures with other firms can advance a major corporation's marketing efforts.

■ The reason that I want to obtain an MBA is simple. I have reached a level in my company where I'm being exposed to issues outside the realm of my previous experience and training. Should we venture into the promising but risky e-books business? Should we continue to print our titles at our plant or sell it and outsource book production? These are vital questions that need to be answered with great care. I'm flattered that our director would solicit my opinion on these and other difficult matters, but today I frankly feel inadequate to answer them. An MBA will develop the skills I need to answer these questions and enhance my impact.

■ Throughout this journey, I will need to call on a deep but nuanced knowledge of financial theory, corporate policy and governance, and organizational management and strategy. The most effective way to gain this knowledge is by earning an MBA at a program

➡

that has excellent concentrations directly related to my private equity focus.

- Knowing that the University of Copenhagen is one of the best in Scandinavia, Boston Consulting Group had come to explain what consulting and the BCG approach were all about. After its exciting presentation I talked with one of the consultants to learn more about what BCG looked for when hiring. Most of the consultants they hired, she said, were either MBAs or were encouraged to earn one after joining the firm.

- I possess neither all the skills nor the professional network that I need to achieve this ambitious goal. I have very limited experience in budgeting, for example, and no training in preparing business plans, defining financial requirements, or estimating future cash flows. While aspects of accounting and economics can be learned by reading books, self-study is simply no match for the spectrum of techniques, ideas, and cases that an outstanding professor can provide. Similarly, taking one course at a time in a part-time format would mean devoting many years to acquiring a management education. Learning on the job is also inefficient, if not impossible: large companies compartmentalize job functions to encourage employees to build expertise, and start-ups are so preoccupied with tactical issues that education is a low priority. Earning an MBA represents the fastest, most effective, and comprehensive way to address my functional gaps and develop a network.

■ In essence, it is an integrative and strategic perspective on companies that I desperately need to develop. The partners at Nomura I have interacted with all exhibit this unique ability to quickly understand all facets of a business, while at the same time stepping back and forming a holistic assessment. I understand that it takes years of experience to achieve this, but when I asked them whether business school might accelerate this process, each one of them said that their MBA experience laid the foundation for the expertise they bring to bear today.

Why an MBA Now?

Many schools don't explicitly ask the "why now" question, but you should address it, either explicitly or implicitly. The timing issue can often be addressed very briefly, but some schools' goals essay gives you the space to elaborate. And some applicants, especially those younger or older than the norm, may need to give these fuller responses, as the following perfect phrases illustrate.

■ My weight-lifting accident and time as a priest explain why I am older than most applicants. My success in graduate school at Arkansas State—I earned a 3.93 grade point average—demonstrates that my college academic performance does not reflect my abilities. In 2003, I was one of only five engineering students at Arkansas State hired by Wal-Mart from the seventy it interviewed. I knew the value an MBA could add to my career, but I needed to establish my career at Wal-Mart before considering business school. Now that I have proved to myself that I can lead the design of multimillion-dollar logistics systems and manage teams of 20, I am ready to earn the MBA that will leverage my skills to their maximum potential.

- My resolve to make my move toward entrepreneurship was hastened last year by two factors. First, the recession plaguing the U.S. economy has actually accelerated outsourcing to Asia and opened up golden opportunities in the software and systems testing niche. Second, winning permanent residency in the United States now gives me the freedom to set up shop here independently and to obtain student loans for my MBA.

- While I could transfer to marketing at Deere, it would mean starting out in a junior position. Moreover, the agricultural equipment industry is extremely cyclical, and its acceptance of the outsourcing paradigm has been frustratingly slow. At age 30, with eight years of fast-track experience, there is no reason for me to postpone earning the MBA that will enable me to switch careers and industries.

■ Why did it take me so long to realize I needed an MBA? First, I received my green card only in 2006, and I knew that without it many post-MBA jobs would simply be out of reach. Second, my daughter, Chia, entered my family's life last December. Because of the care my wife, Mei, needed during her pregnancy I delayed the pursuit of an MBA for another year. Third, I have tried all the alternative paths to my objectives—joining a start-up and striking out on my own—and neither worked for me. All these factors, combined with the sense of perspective that maturity provides, give me a confidence in my decision to earn the MBA that younger applicants often lack.

■ I've spent the last eight years focused almost exclusively on building specialized expertise in real estate development. Because of the complexity and rapid change of this industry, gaining that expertise has required my full attention. It is the indispensable first step in building the credentials and experience I need for a management career in development. Pursuing an MBA before I developed that expertise would have been putting the cart before the horse. In the past year, however, The Rouse Companies' management has made it clear to me that I now have the industry and technical expertise to play a larger role in the company's management. However, my professional experience has not and probably never will enable me to learn all I need to know about running a business unit. I've seen development projects fail because the director or partner lacked the business skills necessary to match her technical know-how. I don't want to find myself in that situation. Today, I have an ideal window of opportunity to gain the management education I need. The demands of my work are manageable, and I am still single and have no family obligations. I now have all the time and resources I need to pursue a degree from the evening MBA program. Because of my age, however, time is of the essence. I must begin my MBA this year. I'm confident that my relatively broader experience can be an asset to my Darden classmates.

Why Our School?

You'd be surprised by how many applicants think that mentioning Wharton's "flexible curriculum, collaborative learning environment, strong alumni network, and brilliant faculty" constitutes a school-specific rationale for applying to Penn. The "why our school" section of the goals essay is all about showing the schools that you've gone out of your way to get to know their resources and their community. The more personalized and face to face your school-specific argument is, the better. We've divided our perfect phrases here into the four general categories you should probably touch on.

General Reasons

- Stanford GSB appeals to me because of its across-the-board general management excellence, its strengths in nonprofit management, its ability to develop leaders, and the rewards of experiencing the GSB's unique community.

- Of all the schools that offer strong programs in social entrepreneurship and global management, Yale SOM's MBA program is the one that offers the best mix of resources to meet my needs.

- I can realize such an ambitious career goal only through a program with Duke's unparalleled cross-disciplinary strength, depth, and flexibility.

- After conducting exhaustive research, attending INSEAD information sessions, and visiting the Singapore campus, I am convinced that INSEAD is the perfect match for my educational needs and post-MBA goals. Everyone I have spoken to who has experienced INSEAD has stressed what a life-transforming experience it really is.

- For me, deciding where to apply has been one of the easiest parts of the application process. I seek a business school with exceptional resources in entrepreneurship, information systems, and international business as well as a program that enables me to stay in Los Angeles. My choice is obvious: UCLA's Anderson School.

Academic Resources

- Kellogg is the best marketing school in the world, and studying with superb scholars like Philip Kotler will give me a state-of-the-art understanding of international marketing. Through such resources as Kellogg's annual Private Equity Conference I can establish the contacts to help me create a Southeast Asian investment fund. From the gatherings of the Entrepreneurship and Venture Capital Club to the Entrepreneurs'"mixers," Kellogg offers the best new-venture resources available.

- London Business School offers the unique blend of resources, foundations-based educational philosophy, and balanced, flexible, and extensive curriculum I need to transition into investment management. London's core classes, which encompass leadership skills as well as managerial and global economics, will augment my accounting background by helping me develop the fundamental functional skills I need to succeed as a portfolio manager.

- "Innovation" may be the latest buzzword at other top MBA programs, but at MIT Sloan it's always been a core value. The New Product and Venture Development (NPVD) track and such courses as "Technology Entrepreneurship" and "Entrepreneurship Marketing" speak directly to my career goals. NPVD's ProSeminar will give me an opportunity to interact with successful entrepreneurs and venture capitalists.

- Wharton's emphasis on Internet-related case studies provides an ideal opportunity for me to refine my business plan. Dovetailing perfectly with my IT background, "High Technology Entrepreneurship" will give me the hard knowledge to start and manage my company. Similarly, "Innovation, Change and Entrepreneurship" will show me how to be innovative, identify threats, and take advantage of the opportunities created by rapidly changing technology.

- Not least, Chicago's innovative and flexible curriculum will enable me to maximize my certainty about my post-MBA career plan by tailoring my MBA to fit my learning needs.

- I want to learn how to write a business plan, financially execute a deal, manage my company and expand it globally, and sell our products worldwide. Courses such as "Managing to IPO," "Start-Up Globalization Strategies," "Formation of New Ventures," or "Strategic Management of Technology and Innovation" will form the foundation of my second-year electives.

- During winter and spring breaks, I intend to participate in the Chazen Institute of International Business's study tours, so I can broaden my exposure to other business environments and cultures.

- Stern Business School is not only world renowned; it excels in the two fields I intend to focus on—management information systems and entrepreneurship. Such classes as "Information Technology Strategy and Management," "Telecommunication Economics and Digital Convergence," and "Technological Innovation and New Product Development" are only a few of the directly relevant Stern offerings I'll pursue.

- Such out-of-classroom resources as the Moot Corp Competition and the MBA Enterprise Corps program will give me the hands-on learning experience I need to succeed as a turnaround specialist. Texas's International Speaker Series and Global Business Conference offer me the opportunity to interact with leadership's best and brightest.

- The constructive feedback I receive from Emory's multiple experiential exercises and role-plays will make me a better leader, and my constructive feedback will hone my classmates' leadership qualities.

- I value Michigan's signature in-company learning model because it will enable me to apply the knowledge I gain in class while I execute and implement real business decisions, all under a professor's guidance.

People: Professors, Students, Alumni

- To succeed, I will need to know how to make the right decisions given limited information and time, exactly the skills our portfolio company CEOs, Zhen Lin and Art Marconi, have exhibited time and again in their competitive industries. Both specifically credited Harvard's case study method with honing this essential skill.

- With over 14,000 alumni in New York alone, my Columbia network will help me establish a sizable customer presence in a city that is home to two of the three largest business districts in the United States.

- Speaking with Ian Killiam (WG '98), I learned how Wharton alumni in Silicon Valley meet regularly to discuss each others' entrepreneurial ventures. I know I'll have access to similarly large, talented, and supportive alumni groups whether I base my firm in Boston, Paris, or Shanghai.

- My interest deepened after having a "Lunch with a Student" in the Arbuckle Cafe, and still more after my long conversations with first-year Shanice Jackson, second-year Akira Suzuki, and alumna Siham Ghabil (class of 2003) about their Stanford experiences. Upon asking them how they would capture GSB in a word, they all said *teamwork*. Talking with members of three of Stanford's student-run clubs—the Out4Biz Club, the Futurist Club, and the Wine Circle—confirmed for me how much collaboration and community really mean at GSB.

- The superiority of Stern's real estate education was graphically demonstrated to me by the dedication of the Stern Real Estate Club. When I e-mailed seven of the club's members with questions, I was impressed to receive five immediate replies. Similarly, Dr. Stephan Brown, the Real Estate Finance Initiative's director, generously took time to describe the superb credentials of Stern's renowned finance professors. Sitting in on "Corporate Finance," I was not only amused by Professor Wurgler's explanation of the origin of the "random walk" theory, but was floored by the sharpness of the students. I left campus totally sold on Stern.

■ To gain the skills and perspective to help Vietnam develop a sophisticated and modern capital market, I hope to study with Yale faculty members, like Roger Ibbotson, who have not only have preeminent expertise in the focus of my future career—measuring and predicting investment returns and risks—but are writing the rules of global investment theory and capital structure theory.

Extracurricular Resources

■ Kellogg's noncompetitive, team-oriented culture is an excellent fit for me. Living in McManus Graduate Apartments with my wife, a current 4Q student, has already made me feel like a member of the Kellogg community. In my visits to the Jacobs Center to attend classes, Social Impact Club meetings, and TGIF social events, I have continually experienced students' selfless, supportive spirit. I am deeply impressed by the willingness of Kellogg students to help others, even during the recruiting season, when job offers are on the line.

■ Since volunteering is a major part of my life, Haas's dedication to public service through its charity fund-raising organization, Challenge for Charity (C4C), and community-oriented student clubs like Net Impact will enable me to continue finding the most effective ways to benefit society while I build my professional skills.

■ Outside the classroom, I hope to start a music club and to create a Carnatic music (Indian classical music) Website to help Carnatic musicians communicate and publish music updates. I may even offer Web-based training in Carnatic music, which my Johnson classmates will be cordially invited to join in on.

■ I feel equally at ease in a classroom, on a stage, or on a ski slope. Since Tuck encourages student participation in both academic and extracurricular activities, I am confident I will find fertile ground for continuing to develop my esprit de corps by joining such Tuck clubs as Women in Business and Tuck African American Business Association. I'm hopeful I will even find other "extremists" willing to organize a group skydiving event—maybe among members of the Tuck Flying Club?

■ From learning and growing with my GSB cohort during LEAD to participating in—and hopefully helping to lead—student organizations like the GSB Soccer Club, High-Tech Group, or Management Consulting Group, I hope to build lifetime friendships with Chicago classmates. As a second-year student, I will enhance the experience of first-years by serving as a student facilitator for the LEAD program.

- Aside from my contribution to Harvard Business School's Soccer, Social Enterprise, and Debates/Public Speaking clubs, I hope to recruit classmates to develop my Dream Charity organization through a second-year field study under Professor James Austin.

- As a past Toastmaster at Wichita State and an invited participant at numerous Java industry seminars and panel discussions, I'm looking forward to sharing my experiences and honing my public speaking skills at Michigan's Toastmaster's club and Improv Club. Through Ross's Habitat for Humanity Builders program, I can continue the community work I began as an inner-city mentor for Miami Cares. Finally, through Michigan's Golf Club I can build friendships while I share both my love of the game and my organizational and fund-raising skills on the club's behalf.

- Indeed, the only negative aspect of Indiana is its lack of a scuba diving club—a fact I plan to do something about.

- Fuqua's rich variety of student interest groups is the direct result of its unique sense of community. The Arts and Culture, Consulting, Finance, Wine, and Investment Clubs—if I can fit them all in!—will all be objects of my attention.

Campus Visits

- My visit to Professor Jonlee Andrews's marketing class earlier this month showed me how successful the Kelley School has been in creating a truly collaborative culture. Students gladly helped each other with assignments, and class discussions were open to all views.

- Singing a Madonna song at the top of your lungs is not an image most people associate with MIT. During my recent visit to Sloan, however, I learned that singing 1980s classics karaoke-style before a room full of Sloanies can be as much a part of the MBA experience as Innovative Leaders and business plan competitions. I had a great time and immediately felt a personal connection with the students I met.

- Spending hours on "Student–2–Student," visiting the Wharton campus four times with my friend, Nellie Glass (WG'09), and attending classes and chatting with students during a 2008 info session in Washington, D.C., have all convinced me that Wharton offers me exactly the welcoming learning environment I seek. During my last campus visit in March, the genuine friendliness of students as they crossed paths on campus and the commitment to fun I found in MBA Pub on Thursdays, Wharton Follies, and the Drag Party at the Pub told me everything I need to know.

- During my McCombs visit on October 18, Ned Ames, my host, explained excitedly how Texas's Plus program uses microconsulting projects and workshops to connect MBAs to companies they're interested in. After learning that McCombs' student clubs include an energy finance group, a Jewish MBA organization, and an MBA card club, I concluded my amazing campus visit by sitting in on John Doggett's entrepreneurship class. I witnessed a great teacher superbly guiding a bright class through India and China's growth strategies. And to think I thought China's brand of capitalism strangled entrepreneurs!

- Walking through wonderful Sage Hall, I was impressed by the Johnson School's open, vibrant community. I was continually approached by students who offered to help me or answer my questions. One even persuaded me to stay an extra day so I could tour the Cayuga MBA Fund's trading facilities! Sitting in on Professor Nir Yehuda's accounting class, I was impressed at how effectively he challenged students to dig further in their analysis of a 3M financial statement. Afterward, I explored what the "SA Johnson Guest Bartending" event really means by dropping by Dino's with three

Johnson students (though I never did figure out what goes on at "Sake & Nails"!). By the time I departed Ithaca Saturday night, I was already dreaming about my next—much longer—visit.

Conclusions

Avoid boilerplate closes. Find a way to echo the themes and details you used in your introduction.

- The operations consulting I intend to do will require me to understand the strategic, organizational, and technical nuances of managing innovation. Because this is the core mission and strength of the Sloan program, gaining my MBA at MIT is the key to my future.
- I'm still amazed by how far I've traveled from that sheet-metal shack in Lagos. With the skills and perspective I gain at Tepper, I know I can travel much further still. I can't wait to get started.
- The challenges I'm confronting today are just the first of the hurdles I'll need to clear to transform InCiVis into the kind of company I know it can become. With the skills and contacts I develop at London Business School, I'll be ready to face them all.
- With a Duke MBA I can be more than just fascinated by the technology of the for-profit space industry—I can help shape it.

- For these reasons, I have decided to make the fourth most significant choice of my professional life—studying at Michigan's Ross School of Business.

- To become the kind of "bilingual" leader who speaks the language and possesses the skills of both nuclear physics and business, I need a program with the rigor, depth, and quality of USC's Marshall School.

- Yet, if I could name only one reason for choosing Columbia, it would be the people—the cream of the crop of 60-plus countries. Among them, I hope to find my venture's future business partners. With them, I know I will experience the ultimate challenge: surviving and thriving through two thrilling years that will transform not just my management skills but my life.

- I now see my life as a journey toward an even broader palette of new friends and new challenges—and UNC Kenan-Flagler as my next stop.

- It's time to take ownership of my longer-term career. Purdue's MBA program will prepare me to do just that.

- Because the other leading business schools cannot duplicate the richness of these experiences and resources, Rochester's Simon School is the only real choice for me.

- I know who I am and where I want to be. I just need the tools to get there. Texas McCombs School offers me those tools and much more.

- These are ambitious goals, but I believe my track record shows that when I am given the resources and opportunity, I reach my highest objectives. I can aim no higher than London Business School.
- Managers who seek the credentials to manage organizations earn MBAs. Leaders who seek to transform their societies earn Harvard MBAs.

Chapter 3 Perfect Phrases for Accomplishment Essays

"What are your three most substantial accomplishments and why do you view them as such?"

(Harvard)

"Describe your greatest professional achievement and how you were able to add value to your organization."

(Cornell)

Accomplishment essays give you the chance to show that you have the skills and personality to affect your environment in major ways. What stories make for strong accomplishments essays? Good candidates are experiences in which your impact was substantial and affected others positively and in which you learned something about yourself or the world. Ideally, they will be recent, nonacademic stories that give the reader some insights into how you deploy your strengths. Often, they will be stories from your professional life showing leadership (even if the school also asks for a separate leadership essay). But nonprofessional examples can also be effective and, indeed, are preferable when you've already used

61

your professional stories in other essays. More than mere descriptions of the actions that constitute your achievement, accomplishment essays should include the following sections:

- Introduction
- Context
- What you did
- Result
- Takeaways

Introductions

- By my definition, a "substantial accomplishment" doesn't have to change the world, but it does have to make you smile every time you think of it.

- My most important accomplishment was a direct result of the biggest—some would say foolhardy—risk I ever took.

- I'll grant you that living doesn't sound like it could count as someone's "most valued accomplishment."

- Failures are the foundation stones of success. I'm proud of two very different achievements because they both took me so close to disaster.

- If "greatest achievement" is defined in conventional terms—promotions collected, deals closed, and so on—then I've done better than starting Tony's Ice Cream Store.

- With six years of corporate life under my belt and a generous severance package to fall back on, I had a rare opportunity to create my own fork in the road.
- When opportunity knocks, it usually doesn't wait around for a reply.
- "Ac•com•plish•ment, *noun*: … (1) achievement, … (2) a special skill or ability acquired by training or practice."
- My three most substantial accomplishments share one common theme: heeding my instincts and having the courage to act on what I believe is right.
- My service in Lima, Peru, as a missionary for the Church of Jesus Christ of Latter-Day Saints was the hardest two years of my life.

Context

- In 2005, I decided to take a break from the hectic pace of corporate life to volunteer for the disabled. Needing a change, I volunteered as a tutor for Laramie College's Special Learning Department, which, though it had more than 30 disabled students needing career assistance, had no formal program to give it to them. Leveraging my human resources background, I offered to design and implement a program to provide these students with access to professional-grade career planning, placement, and course assistance. This proved easier said than done.

■ November 14, 2004. As I was introduced as Procter & Gamble Munich's new sales director, I looked around and saw the same thing in every face: cold fear. Were these the same employees who just seven months earlier were celebrating a 300 percent year-over-year sales increase? Just the day before, however, P&G had dismissed 33 of their colleagues. And here was I, sent from the States by the very same ax-wielding company. "I'm excited to be in Germany; I love your beer," just wasn't going to cut it.

■ "You can do it. You can do it," I repeated to myself as I glided backward across the rink fervently visualizing the gold medal in the state figure-skating championship that was—I hoped—just two jumps and 4.5 rotations away. All I needed now was courage—courage to land the most difficult jump combination attempted in my division: a double axel-double loop.

■ As an engineer at General Electric in 2003, I proposed and created a patentable component serialization device that would automatically insert unique identifying codes on nuclear turbine blade components using infrared laser technology. Integrated with manufacturing production software on the production line, my method would allow turbine component manufacturers to instantly identify defective blades before they passed through the production line. First, however, I had to develop a workable prototype.

- I decided to take the risk of proposing the largest deal, estimated at $400,000, in our company's history.

- My years tutoring high school kids inspired me to volunteer as a night counselor at Newark's Second Chance Club when I was 19. Every day for three months, I faced 50 emotionally troubled, sometimes violent teenage boys. I had to enforce curfews, put out fires, sometimes even prevent them from killing themselves. My most important role, however, was educating them and being accepted as their big brother.

- Three months into the $10 billion merger negotiations between Devus Networks and Shelburne Metrics, a disagreement over valuation caused a deadlock. Merrill Lynch had assigned me, a second-year analyst, to Devus's team without an associate (unusual for high-profile transactions).

- My risk-taking started early. When I was in the eighth grade, my family decided not to take our annual trip to my aunt's house in Hisarya, a small Bulgarian town renowned for its sweet grapes. Disappointed by the break with family tradition I planned and executed a 200-mile bike trip to my aunt's house through a mountain tunnel and over unfamiliar, heavily trafficked roads. I wanted to learn how well I could do on my own under tough and risky circumstances. Though I was young, I shrewdly developed a contingency plan in case I got lost, including a detailed map and a list of hotels and telephone numbers. At 6 a.m. on an April morning I set out.

What You Did

- Back in the United States, I asked friends and family to help me finance all the nonprescription medicine on the list, which cost about $4,000. Although I was able to raise the amount once, this was not possible on an ongoing basis. I therefore needed a new financing partner, which I quickly found: doctors and pharmacists. Of the 32 doctors and pharmacists I visited, 20 were willing to send something from their abundant supply of medicine samples to Dr. Kimbali.

- After discussing the likely needs of the solutions groups with the marketing engineers, I queried the hackers from the security software teams about potential hazards. I then had Oracle's legal department evaluate the intellectual property ramifications since we hoped to use public, open-source software. Last, I helped the program managers plan for the software release. Once the business requirements were set, I led a team of 28 engineers through the standard software development cycle.

- In February, I helped organize HelpNow's first event, a fund-raiser, in Milwaukee. I personally lined up corporate sponsorships, sold more than 50 event and raffle tickets, and hunted down potential items for the gift bag and auction. After my company, Rockwell Automation, declined to sponsor the event, I wrote a letter to the head of corporate communications and then met personally with her to persuade her that Rockwell's $5,000 donation would be benefiting an important cause. When she finally agreed, I contacted the major local banks, including Marshall & Ilsley and Associated Bank, to persuade them to donate similar amounts to the fund-raiser.

- I began my first company when I discovered an opportunity to outsource printing and publicity services to the government of the Illocos region in the Philippines. Placing a printing machine in the basement of its central office, I provided comprehensive and confidential printing services that enabled the government to cut its cost by 35 percent and its print time in half. Initially, my best friend and I were Apo Rizal's only employees, but since our arrangement worked well, we reinvested our earnings, bought two more printing machines, hired 11 more people, and began to offer design services as well. At one point Apo Rizal handled 100 percent of the Illoco government's printing needs.

- When I requested the income statement and balance sheet for the apartment complex on our land, I discovered that it was among Vermont Rental's most profitable: $5 million in rentals and $600,000 in net income. I then created a detailed business plan that incorporated the previous financials and a five-year pro forma. After much soul-searching, I decided that my energies were best spent on real estate development, not operating apartment complexes. However, my partners were so impressed with my plan that they decided to purchase the complex and operate it themselves. This meant that I would have to subordinate my share of the property so they could obtain a second mortgage, which we finally agreed to after a long meeting. Next came two intense months of negotiation both through our attorneys and face to face. To substantiate my asking price, I conducted a detailed financial assessment of the future profit of the complex, and, coupling it with the land-lease revenue, I calculated a net present value based on a realistic discount rate.

- First, I assembled a team of five diversely talented engineers, educated them on project priorities, motivated them to train one another, and assigned tasks to benefit everyone's short-term career goals. Second, I learned how to integrate WiFi technology—a new territory for LandTel—and, after advising a key router supplier to improve its test process, won its commitment to support us throughout the project. At a critical phase, my team was asked to support several large customers and internal departments. To share the unplanned workload, I persuaded management to add three new engineers. Near the end, when unforeseen quality problems arose, I convinced management to delay shipment by six weeks rather than ship a subquality product and risk recall or bad publicity. After the project's completion, I induced management to surprise each engineer with a huge bonus and paid vacation. I helped the project leader win promotion to manager, an engineer's transfer to Marketing, and another engineer's reassignment to a challenging project.

- I designed a computerized database to manage raw materials because reducing standing inventory lowers costs. I designed and implemented hourly statistical control to increase the quality of production. I also established a record-keeping process for setting production parameters, and I implemented a preventive maintenance program to avoid production downtime. Finally, I decreased by 67 percent the time required to switch the production line from one paper type to another by grouping production batches by roll size.

- Working closely with Gap's business information development team to extract brand performance data, I constructed a quarterly brand performance report that included detailed analyses and performance insights. I also won support for a primary consumer target research study to address our lack of understanding of our customer. To develop a truly effective customized retail marketing program for two key retail customers, I collaborated with the sales force, media director, advertising agency, publicity team, and business information development team to develop a media plan that increased sales by 13 percent.

I reinvigorated Pink Denim's isolated marketing team by building proactive relationships with other internal groups, and I gave my teammates the tools and quantitative foundation they needed to measure their effectiveness and make the best fact-based business decisions.

■ In my first meeting, I told the client's staff that the key to designing a new, successful clinical trial was bringing together all the knowledge that was available to us, especially from the Americans, who had won the FDA's approval in the United States. I then formed a 15-member team consisting of the American experts on the drug as well as the client's European and Taiwanese staff, and asked them all to come to Taipei for the kickoff meeting to devise a new protocol. Over the next five months, I used my bilingual skills and bicultural work experience to synergize the skills of my diverse team members. I created consensus by helping the Chinese- and English-speaking team members talk to each other, and I repeatedly flew and teleconferenced between New York and Taipei to promote the sharing of expertise. To drive constructive discussion, I asked the team members to create a list of the problems that were impeding the drug's development, and I then recast each problem as a positive challenge. I also used the "backcasting" technique to help them visualize a positive outcome to the problem and work backward toward a creative solution. My facilitation focused the team's energies, and the clinical trial we developed renewed the confidence of the client's senior managers in the Taiwanese clinical development team and convinced Taiwan's drug authority to review the cholesterol pill again.

- When I took my first private sector job at *Isshukan Tokyo*, I made the case to management that the magazine should boost its community and volunteer efforts. Good public relations, I reasoned, involved projecting a good public image, and so with my self-created charter in place, I set out to meet with various local NGOs to determine how we could work together in pro bono partnerships. I organized the first *Isshukan Tokyo* delegation to participate in the Tokyo Cancer Walk, a fund-raising and awareness-generating walk through the city, and I secured a major corporate donation to the charity. I also initiated a rewarding mentor relationship between *Isshukan Tokyo* and FreePasokon, a nonprofit community computing center in Chiba prefecture. Working with FreePasokon's director, we created a buddy system in which I arranged for the kids from FreePasokon to meet the editors at *Isshukan Tokyo* to find out how they could best prepare for a career in multimedia. We also offered FreePasokon a boost by profiling it in the magazine as an organization that was making a difference in the lives of urban youth.

Result

- By improving IntelliSoft's operations and marketing strategies, I contributed to a threefold increase in sales during my first year and led the firm to profitability. Furthermore, with a more impressive portfolio of clients, in 2006 we were able to successfully initiate a merger between IntelliSoft and Kissimmee Advertising that has created a $5.2 million diversified advertising/Internet services firm with more than 30 clients nationwide.

- I had convinced PepsiCo that we could double profits in two years by restructuring the distribution system, reorganizing the sales force, and consolidating our plants—which would make our rice brands attractive to our customers again without jeopardizing our pasta or side dishes businesses. By changing the minimum order policy and creating an exclusive sales force for my customers, we exceeded my original objectives by tripling profits in those two years. PepsiCo was so impressed by the results that the new infrastructure I proposed has now been exported to Asia and Europe.

- I delivered the first module, which could have taken us a year to develop by ourselves, in approximately six months. Not only did Gibbons maintain its credibility, but it also enjoyed a 10 percent ($3 million) increase in revenues. In the bargain, we also found a long-term partner. Impressed by my work and analysis, management has since entrusted me with the responsibility for managing our existing suite of CAE products as its technical lead—duties that were formerly performed by a development manager with five to six years of experience.

- The results? Under my leadership BolMusic increased sales by $12 million to $36 million. More important, the precedent I set opened doors for students from future generations to become Warner scholars: two years after I joined Warner Music as a regular employee, I obtained management's approval for funding a company scholarship offered to 10 students every year who have to work to finance their educations. This scholarship program is now eight years old.

- Morgan Stanley had agreed to pay Johnson County $120 million in compensation for providing the poor investment advice that led to the largest municipal bankruptcy in state history. The magnitude of the bankruptcy and litigation was overwhelming: $900 million in liabilities and litigation totaling over $1 billion! As the manager of the project team that achieved nearly $300 million in settlements for Johnson County, I regard this engagement as the most visible accomplishment of my career.

- My product received rave reviews from all analysts and press publications and won several awards, including *Auto After Market* magazine's coveted "Technical Excellence Award." In the past three months alone the MapEnhancer contributed $36 million to MacroGeo's bottom line, and senior management has awarded me the MacroGeo Achievement Program (MAP) award and a generous bonus for executing a successful product launch.

- In 19 months, NMOK's membership rose from 1,000 to 5,000; fund-raising revenue increased from nothing to $210,000; and corporate sponsors grew from nil to include Samsung, LG Electronics, and Kookmin Bank. NMOK became the largest and most influential Korean-Mexican nonprofit organization in the country. With enough funding and a large membership base from which to draw volunteers, I recruited 35 volunteers to create a joint program with the Fondo Unido (United Way) to counsel new immigrants on how to survive culture shock, find jobs, and adapt to mainstream society. For helping NMOK to accomplish its mission, I was elected NMOK's director earlier this year.

- Finally, we delivered the project on deadline, reducing system downtime from five hours per week to three hours per month, saving Maersk $2.8 million over two years, and winning us a $2 million contract to support the bidding system. Moreover, by automating most of the testing for the bidding system, we could propose an incredible service level agreement of four hours for the testing job, which previously took three to four days! As I hoped, I was able to leverage our success on the bidding system project to win Maersk's support for a Quality Assurance Competency Center. We gradually removed the stigma of categorizing testing as a cost, and the QACC is now in its third year as a true win-win for A. T. Kearney and Maersk. It generates revenue of $5–$6 million annually for us and is a boon to Maersk because it provides low-cost, top-notch testing services for every software project that is implemented.

- The climax of the journey came in the early hours of the fifth day when, dizzy with pride and altitude sickness, I reached the top of Mount Logan, a 19,551-foot mountain in southwestern Yukon. It was truly an exhilarating moment. I had faced death, challenged my body beyond its limits, and become one of only three students who reached the summit, creating a new record for Canadian students' mountaineering. As a result, I succeeded in obtaining sponsorship worth $30,000 from companies such as Canadian Tire and Hudson's Bay Company. During the two years I was in the office, I led the Canadian Student Mountaineering Association to the summits of two other mountains higher than 5,000 meters. I also built a 120-foot-high rock wall on campus and created a rock-climbing elective with the help of classmates. Ten members of CSMA won the Royal Canadian Mountaineering prize in 2006, and over 2,000 members joined our club in my two years at its helm. Our club received media coverage for our exploits, and students in other universities applied my approach to establish and develop their own climbing teams.

■ This was a substantial accomplishment for me. First, I had extraordinary responsibility and worked under the scrutiny of both Lehman's senior management and the Japanese government and press. Second, when the deal closed, Taihyo's CEO personally commended me to Lehman's worldwide head of financial institutions, who immediately offered me a promotion to associate (normally reserved for MBAs). Finally, this transaction began the consolidation of Japan's confectionary industry that recently culminated in Taihyo's acquisition of Amai Nihon.

Takeaways

- I recognized that I didn't have to be working in an inner-city clinic in Karachi to make a difference. My ability to understand PIKO's goals and convey them to my team so we could produce a blog that could effectively deliver PIKO's message showed me that I have a role to play as a conduit between business and nongovernmental organizations. As I reflect back on the PIKO project, I have come to realize that partnerships between business and social-minded organizations may actually be the best way to effect social change. Each sector has different strengths, and the combination of resources and abilities can be a powerful vehicle for good works.

- I learned how to do construction estimating and scheduling and gained an understanding of construction contracts and familiarity with local zoning ordinances. Moreover, I was able to interact with subcontractors, engineers, architects, building owners, and municipal officials—the dramatis personae of the industry. Dealing personally with all these individuals showed me what they were like, what their jobs demanded, and how they responded to inevitable changes and problems. This seven-month apprenticeship became not only a foundation but a prerequisite for my career with my start-up, Al Ikram

Construction, a colloquium on the art and science of the construction trade. I knew the only reason that I was standing in that room was because of an improbable confluence of good fortune, good choices, and good work.

■ The experience was valuable to me because I got the opportunity to be a "super fan" of these great masters. Not just limiting myself to autographs, I was actually able to talk to them about their music. This was one of the biggest honors of my life. But it was also my first real leadership experience. I learned that there is no substitute for personal dedication and diligence and that thinking big and raising the bar can produce big results. But the most gratifying aspect of the An Die Musik experience was what made it valuable for others: seeing young students develop, for the first time, a sense of the richness of classical music. Even if only a single student learned to appreciate classical music because of our efforts, I would consider it worth every hour I spent on it. I consider this my greatest accomplishment.

■ Turning around my sister's life is easily my greatest achievement. My active intervention, with support from my family, friends, and doctors, saved Chuntao. Years of coaxing her have taught me the art and value of gentle persuasion, even in the face of irrational suspicion and disbelief. Caring for Chuntao while juggling my career and my own family has been one of the most difficult challenges of my life and almost cost me my marriage. As a result, I have matured considerably and learned to be patient and persistent in the face of great obstacles. While I used to be very independent, I have learned that some problems can't be tackled alone. I joined a support group to learn coping strategies and mobilized friends and neighbors to help Chuntao when I had to travel for business. Most importantly, this experience has given me a profound empathy for sufferers of depression and a deep appreciation for the gift of mental health.

■ I value this accomplishment because it forced me to confront the challenges that CEOs face every day, and I discovered I was equal to them. I experienced as never before the rewards and challenges of leading multicultural teams. And though my partners' seniority could have intimidated me, I maintained objectivity and focused on our goal: serving Piper Jaffray's investors. I never flinched from my obligation to tell my boss that his friend's business was a bad risk if that's what the evidence showed. Finally, I learned that even though my CEO had appointed me team leader, I still had to earn my teammates' respect by understanding the case better than anyone and convincing them that our differences in perspective didn't mean that unanimity was impossible.

■ This leadership experience was pivotal for me because it taught me that when I lack formal authority to execute radical change, I must work gingerly and collaboratively to build the consensus to achieve the change. I also learned that leaders can't just delegate; sometimes they must intervene and show others how to work. Most importantly, I learned that teams are *created*. By listening, mentoring one on one, maintaining enthusiasm, and giving them the freedom to fail, I turned 18 demoralized young analysts into an effective team! The bond we forged during those long days is something I won't soon forget.

■ Winning a staff position as a wound-care practitioner after the Marines was a coup. It meant that I would be starting my civilian career in the main office of the fastest-growing wound-care market in the country. I especially value this accomplishment because I was working alongside national-level experts in my field. While I was competent, I had nowhere near their clinical expertise. My position entailed both sales and clinical services, and since my clinical ability was not the equal of my older peers, to compensate I used business skills I didn't know I had.

■ When I entered the family waiting lounge, Frederique's mother hugged me so hard she nearly knocked me over. In that one embrace, my long years of studying, sleep deprivation, and nights on call suddenly fell into perspective. At 11 p.m. on a Saturday night, when most people are enjoying their weekend, studying biochemical pathways and arcane tidbits of pathology can seem an odd use of one's time. Frederique's mother crystallized for me why I went to medical school: I wanted to make a contribution to other lives. Her hug told me I had.

- My experience at Cantabile Studios has had a profound influence on my professional development. I learned how to grow a small business and keep it growing, how to recruit and retain top-notch employees, how to manage the financial and "cultural" aspects of a merger, how to juggle the complexities of contracts and documentation, and how to learn from mistakes. By leaving an established firm for the uncertain future of a film production start-up I took a calculated risk, but the decision has paid off.

- My experience with Jaime changed my understanding of myself. First, I now know I can make a difference in another person's life and have continually sought new opportunities to do so. Second, watching undiscovered talents like Jaime realize their potential has only increased my own personal drive for continuous improvement. Finally, my experience with Jaime confirmed my longstanding belief that everyone should be given the opportunity to excel if he or she really wants to, regardless of his or her history with other managers. Had I followed the human resource evaluations written for Jaime by previous managers, I might never have had the opportunity to witness his motivation, personal growth, or professional improvement. For every person not interested in continuous improvement, there are a hundred more diamonds in the rough waiting to be discovered. Because of Jaime, I now classify all those around me as "undiscovered, untapped potential."

Chapter 4 Perfect Phrases for Leadership and Teamwork Essays

"Give us an example of a situation in which you displayed leadership."

(Berkeley Haas)

"Please describe your experience of working in and leading teams, either in your professional or personal life. Given this experience, what role do you think you will play in your study group, and how do you intend to contribute to it?"

(London)

W here accomplishment essays can, but need not necessarily, show leadership, leadership essays absolutely must. Through leadership essays schools try to zero in on your management potential by evaluating the quality and impact of your leadership experiences thus far. Teamwork essays try to gauge whether you will be able to collaborate effectively with your B-school classmates and by extension the teams you'll encounter in your post-MBA career.

The following leadership/teamwork perfect phrases are divided into the five basic sections common to these essays:

- Introduction
- Context
- What you did (How you led or facilitated your team)
- Result
- Takeaways

Introductions

- My greatest leadership achievement now houses inner-city children on a modest parcel of land in Wilmington, South Carolina. As the general contractor for the 11,400-square-foot Sister Mariah Summer Community Center, I estimated the contract, scheduled the vendors, managed the $2.8 million in construction work, processed accounts payable and receivables, and provided progress reports to the building committee of the Roman Catholic diocese.

- In my experience, the "uncommon result" that is innovation does not have to be the result of extraordinary people. On a team that is led well, the right mix of similarities, differences, and motivation can produce great new ideas.

- My professional and personal success would have been impossible without leadership skills. At Northeastern

I demonstrated leadership by winning election as vice president of Alpha Kappa Sigma, volunteering to serve as treasurer of Northeastern's physical fitness committee, and guiding young people as a gymnastics instructor. My leadership at Halyard & Davis was reflected in the initiative that helped me attract new clients and the mentoring skills that enabled me to nurture my staff's expertise and careers and win the Admiral's Award for Outstanding Mentoring.

■ I taught myself the biggest leadership lesson of my life when I convinced an Italian scientist to let me join her wireless system department and then built a government-funded, cutting-edge ultra-wide-area wireless research group.

Context

■ As the project engineer for Mitsubishi's $1.75 million plant expansion project in Kuwait City, I found myself in charge of eight Indians and one Kenyan, in addition to the Kuwaiti contractors. It was the first time I had led a multinational team professionally. I could see in their eyes (especially the Indians') that they were wondering why I—a foreigner nine years the junior of the youngest team member—had been chosen. Somehow I had to get them to think of themselves as a team and discover ways to motivate them.

■ As union workers, Ford's line workers do not live in fear of their managers. Hence, supervisors who do not know the union rules, are too autocratic, or just rub workers the wrong way are given a form of union hazing that has ruined management careers. I knew at the outset of my six-day test in October 2005 that as an Asian female college graduate I was starting off different from the typical line worker in at least three ways. If I failed to mesh with them, I could potentially be held back professionally and my hopes of being invited into Ford's Young Manager Training (YMT) program for high-potential managers would be dashed.

■ Within weeks of Lawn King's outsourcing of its customer service operations to India, some of our customers began complaining about our customer service—calls were answered rudely or in poor English, applications were being processed slowly, and so on. Though my role was mainly business development and marketing, Lawn King sent me to Chennai to get the customer service representatives (CSR) back on track. The CSRs and I could not have been more different. They were 13 veteran, Indian employees with rural backgrounds, no formal education beyond college, and an average age of 36. I was the young, inexperienced, graduate-degreed African American from headquarters sent to make their lives more difficult.

■ "Dieter, we are counting on you." With that, Hans Pfeiler, Dresdner Bank's head of Pacific Rim financial institutions, charged me with leading the five-member execution team on a $2.5 billion "deal of the year" in spring 2007—the acquisition of New Zealand's fifth-largest bank, Grindlays Bank, by Australia's Commonwealth Bank. After an associate's departure two months before, I was the only person on my Dresdner Bank team who had any execution experience with Oceanian banks. Suddenly, I was in charge of virtually everything: ensuring that the deal's tight deadlines were scrupulously adhered to; taking personal responsibility for all the quantitative analyses; and interacting closely with very senior management, including Dresdner's head of global investment banking. Most pivotally, however, I was given leadership of teams in Berlin, Sydney, and Wellington.

■ When GamePlayer fully acquired 3-DGeek.com in 2005, I was invited to GamePlayer's Silicon Valley offices to assume the daunting task of seamlessly melding the marketing staffs of two complex market-leading companies and three completely different products. The idea that the marketing chief of the smaller "acquiree" should appear at the larger company's headquarters to transform its marketing function was greeted with deep suspicion and even fear. That he would be commanding the activities of staffers typically 10 to 15 years more experienced made a challenge seem like a crucible.

- "Our company has never had a Baltic presence, so we need your team to develop a Web demo—robustly localized, of course—for the local team. Your project manager is located in Tallinn." With these—and only these—instructions from my vice president, I began leading six other newly hired consultants in the strategic planning and development of a $500,000 Web portal for our new Estonian office.

- In February 2004, I became the third employee of Dubey Partners—a two-month-old wireless-focused venture capital firm. After two high-profile months following the firm's first successful incubation project, we were receiving more than 20 business plans weekly and needed more staff. We decided to hire part-time business school students, who commanded one-fifth the salary of full-time professionals. By June, we added five such analysts to review business plans, research the U.S. wireless sector, and develop internal businesses for spin-off. While the students were bright, they lacked training and discipline, and I had only five weeks to turn coal into diamonds.

- In 2007, I cofounded the Bucharest University Consulting Group, a nonprofit student organization providing pro bono consulting services to local businesses and educating students about the profession of consulting. Overcoming the cynical view that the student body would prove too apathetic, I recruited a diverse group of 70 members. However, though students were quick to utilize our career resources, the majority hesitated to commit time to the consulting engagements—our core mission. Our club had hit bottom. Because of a massive layoff, we had lost many members, and as the quality of our meetings deteriorated, so did our learning and morale. We tried to recruit members through e-mail and fliers but with little success. As the club's newly elected president, I sensed an urgent need for change, but I knew that any changes I championed had to appeal to our members' needs.

After several months, I began to notice that Bob's behavior was becoming strange. He repeatedly showed up late for work, complained about being bored with his duties, and protested to his coworkers that he wasn't appreciated. He became moody, withdrawn, and argumentative. I remember thinking, "He's just a little distracted. Silicon Valley is full of odd personalities, and since Bob is such a good employee, I'll just have to find a way to accommodate his idiosyncrasies." But over the next three months Bob's interest in his work seemed to slowly vanish. The quality of his work declined, and he was slow to complete tasks I assigned him.

Leadership or Teamwork Philosophy

Often you'll have space somewhere in these essays to directly state what your management or teamwork style is. Here are some relevant perfect phrases:

- I view leadership as more art than science—there are no universal rules. Only leadership principles that are flexible enough to fit individual cases can succeed consistently.

- Listening is the best way—perhaps the only way—to reopen effective communication.

- I try as much as possible to create open teams, where communication is inclusive and there are no secrets. I also listen more and more to the workers I lead and try to break down artificial barriers. For example, I create nonhierarchical environments where formal labels like "Programmer Rohit" are replaced with first names alone.

- To be successful, a leader must have a clear vision and convince the other people inside the organization to share his or her vision. I address everyone's fears through attentive listening, positive feedback, coaching, and getting people involved in the planning and testing phases. When conflicting interests arise, I gather all the interested parties and negotiate a compromise.

- To be a good leader, you need to command respect. To merit this respect, you need a strong knowledge of the subject matter, a desire to get the job done without regard to who takes the credit, humility and friendliness, and an interest in seeing your teammates learn and advance. People who possess these characteristics tend to be respected and are therefore natural leaders.

- Good team dynamics are never easy, but I have learned that as long as the desire for a solution is there, the solution itself is never far behind.

- In the Kiswahili dialect of Bantu, the word "Utu" is used to describe human relations and can roughly be translated as "humanity toward others." The resonance of this powerful word is best captured by the Zulu saying: "umuntu ngumuntu ngabantu," or: "A person is a person through other persons." This wisdom defines my leadership philosophy.

- As one CEO I worked for once put it, "I spend most, if not all, of my time on decisions that have the potential to sink or save the ship." What he meant was that if a decision is not of paramount importance, he either spends very little time on it or he trusts his direct reports to make the right decision. I will take the same approach.

- The keys to my success as a leader have been "four I's"—inspiration, integrity, initiative, and innovation.

What You Did

- When my new teammates began resisting my early attempts to delegate, I created a climate of trust by reassuring them that I wasn't trying to take anyone's place and by using the Mandarin I knew to show I was willing to meet them more than halfway. To establish productive one-on-one relationships, I eliminated hierarchical barriers and invited team members to talk about whatever bothered them, professional or personal. By convincing them to play soccer and dine together occasionally after work, I fostered a team spirit, and when social/educational tensions arose between teammates, I went out of my way to show them I would treat everyone the same. To motivate work-shy team members I appealed to their sense of pride rather than confronting them directly. When team members became moody, I energized them by talking about subjects they were passionate about—like soccer—until their excitement spilled over to their work.

- First, I coordinated my administrative staff with the orthodontists' staff to cut through the insurer's red tape. To keep my staff from chafing at this extra work, I explained the crucial role they would be playing in bringing much new revenue to the firm. Then I persuaded my superior that this short-term expense would almost certainly boost our long-term revenues and convinced his superior by guaranteeing any losses against my own salary. Finally, I made calls every hour (literally) to coordinate the efforts of the Miami-based manufacturer with international parts suppliers and my New Jersey staff.

■ Two problems stood in the way of effective motivation. First, because my team members told me they felt distanced from management, I proposed and organized a monthly firmwide meeting where our management team could share the latest portfolio developments and new investment strategies. My team members soon felt more involved and gained a big-picture perspective. I also persuaded the head of each portfolio company to speak at these meetings, despite tight schedules, because I believed that a board-meeting format would make junior employees feel like part of management and encourage them to take ownership of their work. The second motivation problem was the feeling among some recruits that their job was just a springboard to other big-name consulting firms after graduation. So I convinced our partners to develop career-track positions with benefits packages, and I designed a performance-review system and a mentorship program. By assigning each recruit to a mentor who was ready to discuss career development issues, we were able to effectively develop and retain people and maintain a high level of motivation.

- Before I could change the customer service reps' perception of headquarters, I had to change their perception of me. To gain credibility, I banished myself from my third-floor office, began listening in on customer calls, helped process applications with the reps, and scheduled several anything-goes brainstorming sessions where they talked and I listened. What modifications would they make to customer service if it was their decision? Because many of their ideas involved issues I hadn't even known existed, I asked more questions and kept listening. I was careful to make no promises, but I told them honestly that I would give their suggestions thorough consideration. I selected the suggestions they had made that I felt were negotiable (e.g., not adopting call scripts) and then lobbied management to accept their suggestions. I also instituted performance metrics and incentives and began assigning them clearly defined objectives.

- By marshaling all the facts and working sensitively around the cultural tensions, I gradually led the "star" team to a unanimous decision. Because Americans are sometimes perceived by foreigners as arrogant, I behaved in a more conciliatory manner. Since the Japanese were naturally excited about keeping Chichibu Resort Japanese, I worked hard to help them see beyond their national pride to the cold, loss-leading facts. When my American colleagues' strong personalities collided with the Japanese's thoughtful diffidence, I had to maintain the spirit of balance. And though my partners' seniority could have intimidated me, I maintained objectivity and never forgot our goal: providing our client with the best possible advice and transaction leadership.

- I started the sessions by summarizing the race. I focused mostly on what we had done right but also briefly mentioned where we could improve and what specifically I thought we should work on. After I finished, I would open the floor to other team members and invite them to talk about the race from their perspectives. Almost more important than what we said during these meetings was establishing a positive tone and demonstrating that I considered each of my team members to be equally important. I wanted each and every one of us to feel responsible for any failure we endured or success we enjoyed. If everyone felt that he or she was individually accountable, then the temptation to blame, accuse, or lash out at teammates would dwindle. Through this process I showed my team that by putting a positive spin on our conflicts and disagreements, we could grow as a team and come closer to our long-term goal of winning a major championship in the next five years.

- I also established a positive tone and demonstrated that I was a hands-on supervisor. I greeted my employees with a smile at the start of the day—5:00 a.m.—and made sure I walked the line to ask the production supervisors how things were going and what they were running short of. My management style was firm but sympathetic. If an employee came in late, I would let him know that he needed to get in on time; and then I would ask if everything was okay at home.

- To correct the situation, I decided to eliminate the administratively tedious task of seeking "real-time" approval from me for everything. Instead, I now encouraged collaboration among team members. Staff members could make a decision and later inform me of it. I also scheduled daily meetings so people would have an opportunity to communicate directly. By loosening my grip and providing a forum for discussion, I was able to supervise the team's progress, yet give my bright, talented, and motivated team members the freedom to complete their work and to make front-line decisions on their own.

- My strategy with Bing and Tom was one I have found to be extremely effective when dealing with other competitive individuals—offer to take some of their work. This approach was magically effective for me in the army. During a grueling forced march in boot camp, for example, one of my fellow recruits was "falling out"—that is, about to drop out of the hike. To lighten the recruit's load, I took some of his gear away and carried it myself. Confronted with the embarrassing possibility that he might need someone else's help to finish the hike, the recruit quickly regained his determination, took his gear back, and finished the exercise on his own without further encouragement from me.

■ My challenge was both to make myself a valuable source of knowledge for my team members and to ensure that they had enough expertise in these technologies and markets to build an accurate budget. First, I developed a knowledge base drawn from our successes in Greece and my business development experiences. Then I initiated regular "knowledge transfer" sessions so we actively learned from each other. My teammates told me they appreciated my commitment to their learning, and it was obvious to me that this knowledge sharing kept them motivated and helped us to build a better budget.

Result

■ My six days on the line met the three conditions for success: no workforce problems, the line kept running, and no personality conflicts with the workers. That ensured me a place in the management training program. But I also received an added bonus: on my last day the tough, unsentimental, "antimanagement" union workers who could have ruined my career bought me gifts and formally requested that I become their permanent supervisor.

■ Within three months, we achieved that goal by improving our productivity sevenfold and saving 70 percent of our outsourcing budget by doing projects internally. Management singled us out for praise, and I received the Colleague Recognition Award from the department vice president, who also gave me responsibility for transferring our new technologies to other departments.

■ My newly unified team's work on the merger reduced costs by 24 percent, the highest ever in Israel, but we also retained top talent and provided generous payout packages. Our cutting-edge joint treasury infrastructure for the merged companies' operations also helped us save $18 million. By leading the merger inclusively, I minimized hostility, and my clients quickly united as one company, viewing me as a friend rather than an enemy.

■ During my first project with Alcoa, I continued to demonstrate leadership but now under the explicit title and role of manager. I scheduled and staffed the engagement, provided guidance to our team during fieldwork, led conference calls with Alcoa's vice president, and performed final quality-assurance reviews of the client deliverable. This first engagement itself generated only $100,000 in fees, but it created the confidence and goodwill Alcoa needed to offer Booz Allen & Hamilton significant new work.

- Over the next two months, wait times on application approvals fell by 35 percent, and our customers began complimenting us on the enthusiastic helpfulness of our service reps. Though on a human level, the reps and I remained very different people, I ultimately won their acceptance. They each greet me like an old friend now when I call in as a customer, and my visits to Detroit are relaxed, upbeat affairs.

- We beat our own deadline by an entire week, earning ourselves a reputation as "the team that can cut scheduled prototype development time in half." One month later, Sumiko called to say that Delhi Partners had won the contract.

- Because of the kind of team environment I helped create as internationalization engineer, between 2006 and 2007, the percentage of GPSWorks' revenue from non-U.S. products grew from 23 to 40 percent, to $44 million. By developing personal relationships with my team members, software developers, and localization engineers overseas, I have helped GPSWorks grow its international market share by 10 percent and reduce the delay between the release of English and foreign-language products from six months to one. Is there a better example of what teamwork can achieve?

- Within three months of my arrival we won two major deals for over $9 million and have since grown our business over 200 percent. More importantly, those petrified looks I saw on my team members' faces when I first arrived have relaxed into smiles of confidence and trust.

- The net result was a happier work environment in which productivity rose by 20 percent. Customers and clients commented on the difference they could sense in the service we provided, and our staff turnover essentially dropped to zero. Most interestingly, as our staff today grows by 10 percent per quarter, nearly all of our new-hires have been referred by current employees. They simply want to give the great gift of working at Virtual Magic to their friends and associates!

- By creating a productive team environment despite a distant manager who was rarely available and a thought leader who was distant in every other sense, I was able to prepare on time the report that met the expectations of our customer, who credited us with its 25 percent sales gain. The same client has since ordered over $1 million in new business.

Takeaways

- The experience taught me that leadership is about establishing common ground to achieve a broad objective. Believing in your cause is vital when the going gets tough, but you can't let persistence turn into stubbornness. Most important, when you cannot get all your solutions adopted, focus on implementing the most important ones. Finally, do your homework. Steven Covey has said that, "Humans have the unique ability to choose their response." When I chose to respond in a manner that improved the environment around me, I realized the true meaning of leadership.

- This experience made me realize that leadership is more than increasing the return on your investment; sometimes it's just a matter of keeping your word.

- This leadership test taught me the importance of diplomacy, having distinct goals, and showing enthusiasm in an environment where my leadership was initially unwelcome. I learned to value the opinion of my subordinates and that unique problems don't deserve prefabricated solutions. I also discovered that few motivational tools work as effectively as making people feel appreciated.

- I discovered that working to make environments fulfilling for others is an outstanding way to make them fulfilling for yourself. Finally, I realized that if I can manage a unionized workforce under the stipulations of the Ford-UAW contract, I can manage anyone.

- Finally, I have learned that my effective leadership "modes" can include organizing, evangelizing, and a small bit of nagging. Though I never thought of myself as a fund-raiser, I see now that I have two of the key traits—the ability to be nice and demanding at the same time.

- This experience convinced me that effective leaders share three key components: (1) they know how to provide direction by defining feasible strategies and vision; (2) they have the ability to motivate by affirming their people's responsibilities and accomplishments and by applying incentives; and (3) they are able to organize and support their teams through efficient work processes and appropriate training.

- I quickly learned that the same management style could elicit different responses in people, so the key was to quickly discover each individual's driver. Some employees responded favorably to me because I was "down in the trenches" with them while others responded only after they saw that I was competent.

- The team-building lessons I learned in South Africa are directly relevant to my Allegro Partners project. First, I realized that no matter how important diversity can be to a team, some key traits must be shared by all: respect, strong work ethic, and positive thinking.

■ Successfully improving the software development process in this project taught me to motivate my team with the tangible benefits, such as flash bonuses, that mattered to them and how to negotiate for resources by describing my team's workload effectively. I also recognized the heavy sales component required to lead change. I learned how to be very persuasive and back up requests to senior management by showing cost benefits. When another team lead tried to destroy the productive environment I had helped create, I learned how to address such disruptive elements promptly.

■ What did I learn? To be effective as a leader and to be seen as one by others, you have to pay your dues in the organization, develop broad skills, and network and build alliances. But most of all, you must identify deeply with the organization's mission.

■ I learned that giving up ground is not as glorious as leading a charge, but leaders need to do both, and that being honest about retreating is better than selling the retreat as a win.

■ While the teams in Tokyo, Hong Kong, Sydney, and New York were viewing the deal from legitimately different perspectives, I learned that someone needed to be "culture neutral" if we were to achieve consensus. I also

➡

learned that even if senior management had given me unambiguous authority for the deal's execution, I still had to gain my teammates' respect by backing up my every statement and convincing them that unanimity was possible.

■ This experience in initiative, innovation, and information-sharing taught me that sometimes an outsider can see—and solve—problems more clearly than those who have lived with them day in and day out. It's also shown me that leadership isn't always about being the manager with the most visibility, largest staff, or biggest title. Sometimes it's about quietly driving change and efficiently revising perceptions.

■ All my teamwork experiences, whether personal or professional, have taught me one overriding lesson: communication is the most important tool when building any team. The better I know my team, the better results the team produces. In learning that, I also realized that McKinsey's Marvin Bower and I have at least one thing in common: we know that leadership isn't about yourself.

Part III

Personal Topics

Chapter 5 Perfect Phrases for Self-Revelation Essays

"Please provide us with a summary of your personal and family background. Include information about your parents and siblings, where you grew up, and perhaps a special memory of your youth."

(UCLA)

"Each of our applicants is unique. Describe how your background, values, academics, activities and/or leadership skills will enhance the experience of other Kellogg students."

(Kellogg)

"What matters most to you, and why?"

(Stanford)

"Outside of work I …".

(Kellogg)

"If you could have dinner with one individual in the past, present, or future, who would it be and why?"

(Berkeley Haas)

In one form or another, virtually every business school requires an essay that forces you to write not about your career and professional experiences but about who you are as a person. Such self-revelation essay topics can vary a great deal in their wording, but generally they can be divided into four broad categories:

- Autobiographical essays: Your family, background, and childhood.
- Values or "what matters most" essays: The values you hold dear and what's most important to you.
- Extracurricular and hobbies essays: What you're passionate about outside of work.
- People, places, and things essays: The individuals you've been influenced by, places you care about, and possessions you value.

Before looking at perfect phrases for these topics, let's consider some introductory perfect phrases for self-revelation essays of whatever type.

Introductions

Because self-revelation essays are so common and so important, we've included some perfect phrases for five types of self-revelation essay introductions. Let your themes, essay material, and creativity suggest the introduction that works best for you.

To-the-Point Introductions

- I am not an easy person to describe.
- What matters to me most in life has been continually expanding as I've grown older.
- In Mandarin Chinese the name Huiliang means "kind and good."
- Musa Qala, Afghanistan, is a long way from Van Buren County, Arkansas.
- It has taken me a long time to decide to write about my father's death.
- For me, the true meaning of honor will always be associated with the small Korean town of Yechon.
- Bruce Bannister was everything I was not.

Quotations as Introductions

- "In life, there are six things, which cannot be foretold with any certainty: Life, Death—Honor, Disgrace—Profit and Loss" —Guru Gobind Singh Ji
- "Am I there yet?" I heard the resident ask behind the curtain. "Do you still see bone on the drill?" the physician replied matter-of-factly.
- "That could be me." A boy in tattered dusty clothes, about seven years old, scampered up to the taxi window as my cab wound its way through Chau Doc, my hometown in Vietnam.

- "What's it like being the daughter of the secretary of state?" the journalist asked, thrusting his microphone in my face.

Scene-Setting Introductions

- June 14, 1992, was a typically steamy summer day in Vientiane, Laos.

- We'd been warned to leave town early, but even 5:00 a.m. wasn't early enough. The gathering mob had beaten us to the station and was making sure no buses got out.

- It was twilight by the time we reached the top of the craggy cliff. I was glad I had dressed warmly, for the Finnish coast can be chilly even in midsummer.

- It's the early 1980s, and as you make your way down the streets of San Francisco, a child flashes by you on a blue Schwinn. As your eyes focus on her receding form, they immediately latch onto a vivid orange shape perched gingerly on the girl's shoulders. It's highly likely the girl you just saw was me, and that orange shape would have been my parakeet Tolstoy, who accompanied me everywhere I went.

- I watched in fascination as Uncle Zhen, deep in thought and grunting occasionally to himself, moved strange pieces around a board of black and white squares.

- Like any other test day, I was extremely nervous on April 23, 2004, and I had barely slept the night before.

- There I was with my aborigine mother and my newborn, half-Mexican daughter standing in the deli section of a department store in Dalian, China. Eight pairs of astonished eyes were staring at me and Juanita, who was excitedly flailing her arms at a row of freshly roasted ducks.

Attention-Grabbing Introductions

- The street in front of me was a war scene of battered cars and torn-up street signs. Baghdad? Kosovo? Actually, it was Allston, Oklahoma, the day my best friend died.

- When people ask me where I'm from, I'm never sure what to say.

- Riding on our school bus through downtown Mosul, my friend Khalid and I were discussing a football match when suddenly the window dazzled with light and a jarring explosion rocked us back in our seats. Then the noise became insane: alarms, alerts, bombs.

- On May 28, 2000, my life was changed forever when I swerved to avoid a metal frame hurtling toward my windshield and sent my Harley careering down a ravine at 60 miles an hour. The next thing I knew, I was being told that I had broken my neck at the C–5 level and would never walk again.

■ Visiting my home one day, my friend Maho laughed and said, "You really do love penguins!"

■ "Wipeout!" The shout of warning ahead of me told me that the Cypress Hill Trail had claimed another Irvine Cycling Club victim.

■ I'm a complete addict and I admit it. Spending my paychecks collecting colorfully shaped pieces of gummed paper may seem an odd hobby, but examining the art that appears on these vivid, sticky-backed shreds is my bliss.

■ They say that dead people can't cry, but I know better.

■ When I was six years old, my family almost traded me away for a boy.

Autobiographical Introductions

■ When I was a little girl, my dream was to grow up and marry the king of Liechtenstein.

■ When I was 10, I accepted a "dare" from a friend and consumed 298 M&M's in the space of nine and a half minutes. I still can't say which was the worse punishment: my violent bellyache or my parents' scolding.

- Two years ago, I stood by my daughter's hospital bed and gave her a kiss goodbye, believing I would never see her again.

- Of the 32 Marines shipped to Beirut with my father on September 15, 1982, only he and two others returned alive seventeen months later.

- My father has been dying slowly for years. I've spent most of my life watching him deteriorate, losing the war of attrition against the unrelenting logic of his brain chemistry.

- I will never forget the sinking sensation I felt every day when my neighbor's mother dropped me off at home— or the night my anxieties proved all too justified.

Autobiographical Essays

Autobiographical essay questions may seem to invite the conventional "I was born in … " response, but steer clear of such kitchen-sink chronologies. Focus on two or three significant themes, experiences, or influences from your precollege life, ones that capture what's unique about your family and upbringing. Let's look at some autobiographical perfect phrases:

- Growing up as an only child in a strict Jewish Armenian household, I was the main focus of my parents'

attention. But that didn't mean I was pampered. I grew up with the strong expectation that I would succeed academically. For high school, my parents sent me to a private school to gain the "discipline" and academic rigor I would need to gain admission to a good college. Unfortunately, I hated the school, which was an all-female private institution in a conservative London suburb. As an Orthodox Jew, I was criticized and teased by other students for "not believing in God" (an absurd untruth) and for my less than total enthusiasm for athletics. Excluded from the social scene, I became more ambitious academically and graduated at the top of my class.

- I am a product of the new India, a mixture of my grandfather's feudal caste system and the progressive culture of technologically modernizing India. Born and raised in the small eastern India town of Nayagarh, I grew up with the burning desire to emulate my father, the gregarious, big-hearted owner of an agricultural equipment plant in our town. When he suffered a fatal heart attack on my thirteenth birthday, I was incapacitated with grief.

- The childhood memories I cherish most are the summer vacations we spent with our grandparents at their country farmhouse near Madrid. My grandfather, now 86, was a fanatical supporter of Francisco Franco, and, after getting howling drunk, would excoriate the "republicanos" with such bitter contempt that even I, a political innocent, felt fear. Yet despite his nightly rantings, our summer holidays with Grampa Federico were true idylls. My sister, brothers, and I would spend entire days wandering among the vineyards, climbing trees, and chasing goats. It was my first lesson in the truth that love and hatred, the dark and the light, can go hand in hand.

- My father was born in northern Quebec but moved to Manhattan in his early twenties where he met and eventually married my mother. While I was finishing my first year in elementary school, my parents decided to return to school and sent me to live with my grandparents for three years in a small agricultural town in Quebec. Because I was already bilingual when I arrived, this was not a big change for me culturally. But on a socioeconomic level it was a true shock. I had traded the comfort and sophistication of the Upper West Side for a barren farm in the ice-caked tundra of the Great White North. Forced to adapt to my severe new surroundings, I quickly became independent, only to be forced to readapt to my old Manhattan life when I rejoined my parents four years later.

- My intense curiosity about the world stems directly from my childhood. Growing up in an isolated valley of the Ch'ang-pai Mountains, I had a burning desire— unsatisfied until I was eight—to see what was on the other side of the mountains that surrounded our home. My father, a tax collector, was the first in his family to attend college, and he raised me to understand the value of education and self-reliance. In 1998, my family and I immigrated to the United States, but when my grandfather fell terminally ill a year later, my parents returned to China to care for him. I was only 17, but I made a gut decision to stay in the United States and fend for myself, against my parents' direct wishes. As a child of a culture in which obeying one's elders is bred in the bone, it took everything I had to disobey my parents. I was on my own.

Values and "What Matters Most" Essays

The danger posed by values essays is twofold: (1) you'll focus on values that are too banal ("balance in life") or broad ("personal growth") to help you stand out from the pack, or (2) you'll forget to anchor the values with concrete examples from your life that illustrate you living those values. Avoid these traps.

The following perfect phrases exemplify some of the value statements that can give these essays traction.

- As I grew and discovered that my childhood world was not "the norm," I took the Midwestern values of hard work, practicality, and steadfastness I had inherited and focused them on creating a different future for myself. I believed, because I had to, that with vision and effort anything is possible.

- The elements of my life that make me "unique" are the personal values of healing and helping that have always been inextricable from my work. The work I do is a direct, unmediated extension of what I believe in.

- My willingness to experience that shock three years ago exemplifies what I value most: continually expanding my definition of myself and understanding of the world so they encompass more people, experiences, and cultures. Whether I do this by pursuing my broad intellectual and literary interests or through my commitment to improving the cities in which I live, I strive to become a citizen of the world in every sense of the term.

- As young as I was, I understood that going to school was the only opportunity I would have to break out of the smothering environment of Shuwayhitiyah, where girls had no choice but to listen to their parents or husbands all their lives. I wanted independence. I wanted freedom: freedom from poverty, freedom from a sexist system, freedom from a system where parents decided everything. This burning desire for freedom has remained the most important theme of my life and will always be what drives me.

- On the whole the relations among my overpopulated family were very good, and I learned the value of tolerance. With so many family members vying for attention, I had to learn that I could not always expect to get everything I wanted. I had to compromise to get what I could. This turned me into a very flexible person with the ability to see things from all points of view and to differentiate what is essential from what is not.

- I am not precisely sure where and how I developed my strong sense of ethics, but choosing to do the right thing has always been a natural instinct for me. When you have strong ethics, people know it, and moral dilemmas tend to pass you by. Even in Pakistan, where corruption is endemic, I personally have never had to participate in it. If I had to bring only one value to Kenan-Flagler, it would be the invisible force of integrity.

- What has mattered most to me in life, next to my friends and family, is learning not to run away from uncertainty and social ambiguities, but to transform them into constructive contributions to society.

- I also realized that what matters most to me has not changed and does not need to. I still believe in family, community, and leadership. The horizon of what motivates me in life has continuously expanded, taking me to the places that as a child I had dreamed of flying to as a pilot. What I wanted most as a boy was to become a pilot and to make my father proud. As a teenager it was my family, my ancestors, education, and the church. After my father's death, it was supporting my family and helping my neighborhood. And today, what matters most is helping my community and helping Cambodia. From the self- and family-oriented concerns of a boy, I have learned to place the most importance on my community and society—those whom I can benefit most through my leadership skills.

■ When my father moved our family from Egypt to the United States in 1989, he sacrificed a solid career, a comfortable lifestyle, and a respected role in the community so my sister and I could receive American educations. I lost my chance to fully thank him for this gift to me when he unexpectedly died of a heart attack in 1997. Although almost 12 years have passed, his ideals of integrity, leadership, and generosity are still the values that guide me.

■ I watched my father travel 120 miles several times a week to earn his master's degree while working full-time for the Indian government. When asked why he worked so hard, he answered: others depended on him; it was his duty. He and my mother's lifelong example of integrity, perseverance, and optimism are the same values I will offer my Rochester classmates.

Extracurricular and Hobby Essays

Another way to show schools who you are is to describe the activities that you're most passionate about. Extracurricular essay topics invite you to do just that. Whether your nonprofessional interests center on rugby, haiku, or astrophysics, you want these types of essays to vividly communicate your love for your hobby. Some applicants' extracurricular devotion centers on social impact activities. Because a few schools have separate essay topics for such volunteer community and social impact involvements, we present perfect phrases for those topics in Chapter Nine.

■ To seek that sense of spiritual rebirth, my husband and I set out on hikes to our favorite campsite, located deep within the Adirondack Mountains. As we ascend the switchbacks, our packs firm against our backs, I feel the stresses of everyday life begin to fall from my shoulders. Out in the wilderness, I find pleasure in the simplest things, from gathering wood for a fire that will warm us once the sun disappears to searching for a flat stretch of land where we can pitch our tent. Whenever I return from a weekend in the wilderness, I feel invigorated and ready to take on the world.

■ In the language of an introductory psychology textbook, I have a high need for cortical arousal. I enjoy cycling, skiing, travel, rock climbing, photography, and flying. My recreational interests tend to evolve and change. For instance, when I first started flying, I derived a great deal of enjoyment from exploring Canada and taking photos. Next year, I am planning to try my hand at aerobatic flying. I am always looking for something interesting and unusual to try.

- Carnatic music is one of the best known of the many ancient forms of Indian classical music. Consisting mainly of devotional songs composed centuries ago to praise the many Hindu gods or to pray for health, peace, and wealth, Carnatic music synchronizes one's body and mind and helps one assimilate and enjoy life. Accompanying instruments such as the violin and miruthangam (a percussion instrument) add flavor to this vocal music, but it can be just as good on its own. It encourages soul-searching and helps me balance my life between temptations and the rational calm that should govern life. Carnatic music also fosters family life. I can almost feel goodness entering our home and hearts when this music is in the air.

- I have gone on to run some 20 races (mostly for charities) and can now endure 18-mile-long runs. I will run my first marathon shortly. My daily runs and occasional races not only improve my physical endurance; they have literally changed my life. I have yet to finish first, but the journey is what it is all about, and it has been a fantastic one. Running has instilled discipline of the highest order in my life. Knowing that I can go the "extra mile" has given me an extra edge and the confidence to succeed in both my personal and my professional life.

- Since the first moment I stood in front of majestic, imposing Mount McKinley, I have been passionate about mountaineering. For all the brute physical skill it requires, mountain climbing is also a very philosophical activity. Like life, mountaineering poses ambiguous choices regarding success and goals. Like succeeding at life, ascending mountains requires teamwork, a bond of trust among the climbers, and shared passion. As a team we decide together by which path to make our ascent, through the tangible bond and symbol of a single connecting rope, we trust our lives to each other. We also decide as a team who will lead the stages of the ascent, and as a team we overcome danger and reach the summit through perseverance, creativity, and adaptability.

- My passion is training to become a minister for New Light Family Church. The purpose of the ministry program is to teach individuals how to develop sound ministries through course work in everything from communication and church administration to biblical history. On graduating from the two-year program, many students seek work as full-time ministers in one of New Light's churches. After months of 35-hour weeks (including homework) on top of a supervisory position that required me to rise at 4 a.m., I was proud to graduate from the ministry program with a 4.0 GPA. At the end of the year, however, it was the bonds I had formed—the team spirit we could all feel—that mattered most to all of us. It gave me firsthand experience in maintaining enthusiasm and camaraderie in a tough, demanding environment. Instead of reacting to the stress by becoming consumed with my performance, I was able to remain conscientious and "honorable" with my classmates.

■ Outside of work I race cars—fast cars. Cars with 24-valve V–6 engines bored out of 3 liters to even 3.3 liters and force-fed with a Paxton supercharger dialed to produce 11 pounds of compressed-air—a boost so hot you need an intercooler mounted on the front to dissipate the heat. The cars I race have suspensions so stiff that my brain literally rattles inside my helmet if I hit so much as an occasional rock on the racetrack, and tires so sticky you'd swear they were made out of chewing gum. Racing is a passion of mine not only for the adrenaline rush, but because of the way it heightens my senses, my mind, and my agility. In a sport where winners are decided by differences of less than 1/100 of a second and where you must react immediately to changing track conditions, racing has greatly sharpened my focus, reaction time, and ability to make split-second decisions.

■ Foxtrot, waltz, tango, quickstep, salsa, meringue, swing, and break dancing were not things I expected to learn when I started college. Signing up for a ballroom dancing class my freshman year, I picked up the basic steps with such ease that my dance instructor thought I had taken classes before. However, I had much to learn, as this form of dance requires a unique and intense mutual understanding between the partners that I was unaccustomed to. Dance requires both people to communicate and work together as if they are the same entity, as one cannot move without the other. Dance has enhanced my experience of life.

■ I once read that a senior teacher used to advise brand-new teachers to leave the field as soon as they started enjoying themselves. Her reason: the fulfillment of teaching is addictive, and like all addictions it is very difficult to break. I know exactly what she meant. Whether I am teaching reading skills to young children through Good Shepherd Elementary or sophisticated hedging strategies to traders, teaching stimulates me intellectually, gives me the satisfactions of public "performance," deepens my capacity to build rapport with people from every background, and enables me to positively affect the lives of my students and the community as a whole. That is a powerful, even "addictive" mixture.

■ I quickly became fascinated by the philosophical underpinnings of our style of karate, di do kwon, a Japanese variant of traditional tae kwon do. I learned everything I could about the principles of sustaining determination and focus, maintaining an unassuming demeanor, and constantly remaining attentive to my surroundings so as to better respond to any situation. The milestones of my journey to my black belt are still vivid: my first sparring match, my first successful spinning heel kick, the first time one of the high-ranking students told me my technique looked good. With each new achievement my resolve to complete the journey grew stronger.

People, Places, or Things Essays

Still another way business schools use to discover who you are is essay topics that invite you to discuss specific people, places, or things that matter to you. Let's look at some perfect phrases for these essays.

People

■ My younger brother has also had a profound impact on what matters most to me. He is an animal activist and the founding member of the Nepalese branch of People for Animals, an organization started in Bombay in 1994. Nepal is a Hindu country, so cow slaughter is banned by law. In defiance of this law, 250,000 illegal abattoirs have proliferated in the country. Most of the cattle is trafficked out of India. My brother helps police apprehend the owners of these slaughterhouses and also teaches people to treat animals humanely. Despite Nepal's bureaucracy and illiteracy, he remains confident that he can have a profound impact on the way people think about animals. I do too.

■ The person who has done the most to shape me through his example is my grandfather, Zhang Wei. Even today, the townspeople of Matang still do not know how he survived the accident that nearly killed him seven years ago. While crossing the street, he was struck by a speeding car and lay in the road for almost two hours before a neighbor found him. Though he lost his leg, he never once exhibited any rage for vengeance. "The driver probably did not see me," he charitably offers, regretting only that running his farm is harder now. When relatives advised my grandfather to sell his farm and move to the city where he could be looked after, he simply declared that that would be like losing his other leg. Everything takes him twice as long now, but even at 74 his farm is as productive as the best in the region.

■ "Let's go see Mrs. Jenns," was Dr. Brian Melman's way of recruiting me for an after-hours house call not too long ago. It was 9 p.m., and we had already been on call for two days. I knew he couldn't have slept more than a few hours because I had been with him. Though 30 years my senior, he looked ready to climb Mount Everest—or pay a house call on a dying patient. Dr. Melman inspires me with his intelligence and clinical expertise but also with his indefatigable attitude. For him, pharmacology, physiology, biochemistry, all the scientific aspects of medicine, are just gateways to the more rewarding subject—helping sick people. About to start my third consecutive night on call, I asked him how he maintains his energy and enthusiasm. "It's easy. As bad as I sometimes feel, and sometimes it's pretty rotten, I know what the patient is going through is much worse."

■ If I were a character in a book, I would be Wu Zetian (625–705 AD), the only woman emperor in Chinese history. To me, she is a heroine and a role model in male-dominated society. I admire Wu Zetian for her courage to be independent minded and fight for what she believed in. A favorite concubine of Emperor Gao Zong, Wu Zetian managed to become his empress, but,

➡

unsatisfied with the conventional submissive female role, she gradually gained control of the court. Empress Wu courageously declared herself emperor of China, and to challenge patriarchal Confucian beliefs, she promoted efforts to elevate the status of women, such as through scholarly biographies of famous women. In spite of the ruthlessness of her climb to power, her rule was benign. She once said that the ideal ruler ruled like a mother over her children. Empress Wu is an example to me of a woman using her unique talents to contribute to society.

■ My brother Jason was my friend, first mentor, and toughest competitor. When he became our state's high school wrestling champion in 1997, I practiced with and learned from him until in 1998 I was able to take the title from him. Jason taught me the fundamental rule of competition—"Play to win, but dare to lose." I excelled in sports and school because of the determination and leadership I learned from him. Telling me, "I want to serve my country," Jason become an air force officer. Although engine failure took him from me 18 months ago, he remains the person I look up to most.

■ My father's company ultimately discovered his secret and labeled him a "Vicious No. 9"—the lowest rank in Chinese society. Asked about his family background, he could have lied, but instead told the truth—my

➡

great-grandfather was an officer at Chiang Kai-Shek's military academy before the communist revolution. Because of his "bad" family background, my father was criticized publicly by his coworkers for days. Fortunately, history has already made its judgment, and my father was right to believe in honesty. My mother once told me that I would understand the values my father stood for when I grew up. My commitment to leadership while at USC and afterward is the best way to show her I know she was right.

- When I started at Armulex, Kathy Dyson was the CEO, and as a new employee in an entry-level job I should have been invisible to her. I was not. She tried to get to know everyone in the company, and whenever she ran into us in Armulex's cafeteria, she would always sit down with us and encourage us to discuss any company issues with her. I was impressed by Kathy's openness and her ability to make her vision our vision through the sheer force of her inspiration. By leading Armulex from its tough start-up period all the way to its initial public offering and then on to its current position as the world's leading printing industry chemicals supplier, Kathy set a personal example for me of how to push the envelope and think outside the box. Under Kathy Dyson, I have learned how to think innovatively and to explore alternative ways to improve existing processes.

Places

- It was the Australian interior's very size and solitariness that drew me in. In 2005 I therefore left the ocean behind and ventured into the outback to meet Australians, encounter Aboriginal culture, and discover the physical beauty of places like Uluru (the Aboriginal name for Ayer's Rock) and King's Canyon. The sparseness of traffic on Australia's single-lane dirt roads occasionally left me stranded without food and forced to spend the night in the desert under the southern stars. But I toughed it out, saw the beauty of the Aborigines' decorative paintings, watched as they performed their tribal dances to the accompaniment of their didgeridoos, and in three weeks strolled exultantly into Perth.

- No sight brings me as much joy as the serene Himalayan ranges. It is nature's most beautiful face. My love affair with the Himalayas began in high school when I first trekked into the Har-Ki-Dun valley, with its surrounding 6,000-meter peaks. I was overcome by the unexploited beauty and grandeur there and returned so often that I made many good friends among the locals on my treks. Though they love their rudimentary lives as farmers, they lack ready access to medical facilities. So with the help of my friends and fellow Climbers and Explorers Club members, I helped set up medical camps in the Har-Ki-Dun. At Purdue I plan to start a mountaineering club that organizes treks into the heart of this breathtaking place.

- I grew up in Bordeaux, a large city in southern France renowned for its rich economic, intellectual, and cultural capital. Bordeaux has the scale, atmosphere, and attractiveness of Paris without the overwhelming aspects of daily life in a crowded city. Bordeaux is also known worldwide for its wine. Saint-Emilion, Pom l, Château Eyquem are only some of the magic names admired by connoisseurs. Just as much as wine, however, I grew up prizing Bordeaux's extravagantly colorful history. In 1154, the duchess of Aquitaine married Henri Plantagenêt, the future king of Great Britain, and bequeathed the entire region of Bordeaux to him as a "gift." So, for three centuries this quintessentially French city was British!

Things

- Because cycling has been my personal passion over the years, my Crumpton SL road bike has become the one possession I value most. Today, I race competitively for a locally sponsored team and train 5–10 hours a week even when I'm on the road. In the summer, I travel most weekends to race with my teammates, who are also my closest friends. Cycling has been a tremendous source of camaraderie in my life, and it taught me my first lessons in teamwork. My teammates and I routinely sacrifice our individual chances of winning to let our strongest rider "draft" off us so he can take his best shot at winning. That teammate repays us by winning the sprint finish. I'll share this same lesson with my Kelley School peers.

Chapter 6 Perfect Phrases for Diversity, Cross-Cultural, and Contribution Essays

"Please choose one phrase that describes you from the set below and support your statement using concrete examples. Professionally I am: (a) involved globally. (b) committed to diversity. (c) socially responsible."

(Virginia)

"How have you experienced culture shock?" (Harvard)

"How would you contribute to our community as a student?"

(NYU Stern)

"How will your unique personal history, values, and/or life experiences contribute to the culture at Tuck?"

(Dartmouth Tuck)

Business schools want diverse classes—period. Fortunately, they define "diversity" quite loosely. Aside from race and gender, your personal or family history, your

133

religion and cultural background, your hobbies and passions, even your sexuality (if handled properly) are all fair game as diversity essay topics.

International or cross-cultural experiences are a subset of the diversity idea. They are desirable for the same reasons: they help you add color and variety to your entering class while preparing classmates for the increasingly globalized workplace.

Because admissions committees often use diversity essay questions to explicitly ask applicants how they'll contribute to their school, we've included contribution perfect phrases in this chapter as well. In business school–speak "contribution" means two things: what set of experiences, qualities, or perspectives do you bring that can add something special to your class and in what specific school forums or activities will you make this contribution? The perfect phrases in this chapter will show you how to strike the contribution chord.

Introductions

- Because preconceived perceptions and assumptions have never applied to me, I know they can't be applied to others. As a child in a multicultural family I learned to appreciate my differences and, by extension, to be sensitive to them in others.

- The diversity I offer Cornell is based on four unique elements of my life: my professional experiences in corporate finance and the hospitality industry; my appreciation for the Persian, Kurd, and American cultures that define me; my quantitatively rigorous education and graduate research work at MIT; and my efforts to fight discrimination based on sexual orientation.

- Homemade pizza, lasagna, southern-style barbecue ribs, Indian fried chicken tikkas, Malaysian-style dessert. You might be surprised at how varied the food can be at a neighborhood potluck party in suburban Amarillo, Texas.

- "We really need a man for that position." Not quite believing my ears, I was forced to admit that discrimination did exist at Beecham Industries.

- The Jingxe Bank branch where I interned at university in Taiwan had 100 employees, and every single one was Chinese. Diversity did not exist.

- In living, working, or traveling in over 40 cities in 15 countries I have learned what Lou Holtz meant by, "If you want to succeed, be uncomfortable." My willingness to be vulnerable to transformation has given me multicultural skills, treasured friendships, and rich memories that have prepared me to lead in a rapidly globalizing marketplace.

- Growing up in Warsaw and attending the French school there for nine years gave me an early and intense taste for cultural dissimilarities that I've since pursued across twelve cities and four continents. Why are Norwegians so formal when they toast? Why is the United States filled with flags? Why do Turks waste so much water? Why are chopsticks plastic in Chinese restaurants, metal in Korea, and wood everywhere else?

- Sometimes the best way to understand the society you belong to is to leave it. As a Swede who loves his country, I've spent an unusual amount of time living, traveling, and working outside it, and it has helped me understand myself and Sweden better. I share Sweden's faith and cultural heritage and believe in its future—which is why I will return to Stockholm after my MBA. However, it is my multicultural experiences in Sudan, Korea, the United States, and Germany that have given me the perspective to feel confident about that decision.

- Eating a hard-boiled egg at the summit of Mount Fuji requires a daring palate and the good sense to pinch your nose ever so lightly to avoid being overwhelmed by the sulfuric odor from the area's indigenous hot springs. This odoriferous treat was my parents' idea of a reward for not complaining during our seven-hour ascent to the revered volcano's crater. But I was most interested in my father's walking stick, branded with a dozen different kanji inscriptions announcing the waypoints along our route. At 10, I was probably too young to appreciate the significance of our trip and our hosts' reverence for the honored "Fuji-San." But the walking stick remains a metaphor for my continuing journey to embrace international cultures and new experiences.

What You Did: How You Showed Diversity or Multiculturalism

- I never expected to "come out" to my coworkers at Lazard Freres. But when volunteering to conduct an AIDS awareness training program for our field offices, my manager asked me the reason for my interest. Since then, while conducting corporate training programs across the organization, I have been pleased to learn that my disclosure has opened dialogue among Lazard employees about gay and lesbian issues in the banking industry.

- Being trapped in the middle of an anti-Shiite riot is one of my most chilling memories. My friends and I, all Shiites from southwest Baghdad, were visiting Fallujah during a training trip. In this war-wracked city, we suddenly became targets as protests against the imposition of Shiite control ignited into full-scale riots.

Our escape involved racing the mob to another bus stop outside town, watching the (fortunately empty) bus ahead of us endure heavy stoning before being overturned and set afire, and entrusting our lives to a courageous driver who miraculously navigated our bus through the mob with only five shattered windows.

- The beauty and complexity of salsa was unlike anything I had ever experienced. After completing my introduction to dance class, I built on my rudimentary knowledge of salsa by taking lessons twice a week at a local dance school. The first three months of lessons were excruciatingly difficult, but I persevered until I achieved a level of expertise that enables me to dance with almost anyone. As soon as I was confident of my ability, I began taking my skills into the "real world" by going to Latin clubs such as the Copacabana, Latin Quarter, and El Flamingo. Naturally, I stand out at these clubs but regard comments such as *bailas bien para un gringo*—"you dance well for a gringo"—as the highest of compliments.

- Within its own borders Iraq was to some extent a unique world of its own: many different nations lived together while retaining their own cultural heritage. I was an Iraqi, a Kurd, and because of my ancestry—a Turkish-born Kurd living in Iraqi Kurdistan—even a Turk. I grew up in a polyglot atmosphere in which I spoke

Kurdish to my friends one minute and Arabic the next while trying to keep my Turkish alive with my relatives. Even today I can express some thoughts better in Kurdish, some better in Arabic, and others more effectively in Turkish.

- These early cross-cultural experiences made me adept at "escaping comfort" and adapting to new environments. I have learned how to lead from VC executives, CEOs like Steve Jobs and Steve Ballmer, foreign ambassadors, and church leaders. I have interacted with poor Indonesian city kids, American farmers' sons, and Costa Rican migrant workers. I have caught (carefully) piranha and crocodiles in Venezuela's rivers, defended gay employees from abuse in a Wal-Mart call center, cataloged Russian Orthodox religious icons for a private collector, and taken a three-month sabbatical to travel in Sri Lanka with a Tamil student.

- As a son of a French-trained World Bank expert in animal genetics, I had an international life virtually from birth. I spent my first five years in a diverse, multilingual research community in Azerbaijan where my friends and neighbors ranged from Azerbaijanis and Russians to Brits and Indians. When I was six, we moved back to Kuala Lumpur. Though I have lived there since I was six, I have continually sought out international experiences.

At 14, I served as a cultural guide for the Burmese team in the All-South Asian Games, and met people from all over the continent. When I was 16, I spent a summer in New York working for Taco Bell, where I gained my first lesson in business and interacted with people from Mexico, Canada, Brazil, and Holland. Spending summers with my father in Brussels, Belgium, when he was relocated there, gave me another powerful lesson in diversity.

- Joining dragon boating sessions organized by the British Chamber of Singapore for the past two years has reinforced my life's diversity lessons in a distinctively Singaporean way. Paddling furiously with Australians, New Zealanders, Canadians, and Swiss, I must be synchronized with my teammates, moving through each phase of the stroke in perfect unity. Though I considered myself to be a physically fit dragon boater, the inevitable fatigue eventually forced me to acknowledge my reliance on my diverse teammates. The experience is always an exhilarating one.

Diversity and Cross-Cultural Insights

Here are some perfect phrases that show how you can step back from describing your experience and demonstrate your insight into the importance of diversity or multiculturalism:

- Strong language skills—I speak Farsi, French, English, and Hindi—are the practical manifestation of a global outlook.
- My dynamic work experiences range from a Korean government agency to an American video gaming start-up, from the world's largest software company to a small family-controlled modem maker. By giving me exposure to many different technologies, functional areas, and business models, these experiences will enable me to be an important contributor to the dynamic case discussions at Darden.
- As a Tokyo-born molecular geneticist and future entrepreneur, I will bring my true diversity to the heterogeneous melting pot of Yale SOM. As a brain research scientist, I break the investment banking/management consulting MBA mold, and my dual-culture life experiences in Japan and Canada have taught me how to view issues from many angles. They have also given me perhaps my most important asset: adaptability, the ability not only to master new languages but to make new friends and meet new challenges.

- While touring a production line on a business trip to Tunisia in 2007 I noticed that my colleagues became much more willing to share information the moment I began conversing with them in Arabic. People are simply more receptive to everything, from a compliment to a suggestion, when it is given in their mother tongue. Today, I am proud to say that in addition to my fluency in Arabic, Greek, and English, I am pursuing proficiency in Chinese, so I can build on the rapport I have developed with my new Beijing colleagues. The power one gains by understanding a foreign language cannot be understated.

- The process of assimilating myself to life overseas has made me a more interesting and versatile person. I have become accustomed to seeing street corners guarded by armed security men, to greeting male and female associates alike with a collegial hug, and to visiting the victims of this beautiful, war-stricken country. It has made me more appreciative of the cultural differences I took for granted as a Russian-Korean American and has inspired me to dedicate my time to two Colombian charities.

Contributions

- INSEAD is like a VC fund that is considering investing in me—it's expecting equity in return. One of my contributions will be my experiences in mobilizing public support to prevent unjust treatment of India's women and lower castes.

- New venture management and risk taking are not just my MBA goals; they are major themes of my career. I offer my Carnegie Mellon classmates the insights of someone who has already faced the challenges of growing ventures. Each time I managed a branch at Wells Fargo I was essentially either starting up a new "company" or reinventing failing operations. Since every branch served a unique community, I learned to create customized market assessments and strategic business plans that would work in each location. One reason I was successful is another skill I want to share with my Tepper MBA class: my experience in building "guanxi"—strong professional networks and productive associations.

- My experiences running for election for India's Bhartiya Janata Party will give my USC classmates rare insights into the realities and concerns of Indian regional politics today. To my Marshall classmates who may manage a company with interests in India, my insights may give them potent leverage during business negotiations with the Indian government.

- Growing up in four different regions of the vast Russian subcontinent, working with Scandinavians and South Americans in London, forming a soccer team in the American Deep South—wherever I have been, I have promoted exploration, open-mindedness, and personal challenge as my guiding principles. I will make a real contribution to UCLA because my spirit of discovery is infectious, and my experiences have taught me a great deal about working effectively with others.

- How will I enrich the learning experiences of my Tuck classmates? By inspiring them to work harder than they thought they were capable of, by challenging them to strive for goals they thought were unattainable, and by demonstrating that we are bound only by the limitations we place on ourselves. My distinct personal and professional experiences will not only contribute to their success; they ensure that my prospects for future success as a leader are high.

- I also look forward to becoming part of Rochester's commitment to creating a diverse learning environment by contributing the many other aspects of my experience and background I have not mentioned here—my friendliness, my team spirit, and my strong sense of responsibility.

School-Specific Contributions

Since contribution essays ask you to describe how your diversity or uniqueness will enhance your classmates' experience, you should explicitly refer to the relevant school-specific resources where you'll make your contribution. Here are perfect phrases that do this:

- When I sampled UNC's unique culture in February, I met students just like me—world-traveling multiculturalists with a zest for leading change. If I am given the opportunity to join this community, I will not only contribute by sharing my international consulting and entrepreneurial insights in class discussions and study groups. I will also enrich Kenan-Flagler's collaborative spirit through my bond-forming participation in its Christian Fellowship, Carolina Women in Business, and Military Veterans clubs.

- At Chicago, I will offer the leadership and teaching experience I gained in the transportation industry to add diverse value in case studies and projects. I intend to help the Graduate School of Business's Operations Management Group grow and accomplish its mission by working to attract speakers and funding to develop courses or research. I want to make Chicago the preferred choice for recruiters from transportation leaders such as UPS, Fedex, and A.P. Møller-Mærsk.

■ At Berkeley Haas, I will channel my varied experiences in pharmaceuticals, hospital administration, and medical research into creating networking opportunities with leaders in the biopharmaceutical, medical devices, and diagnostics industries through the Berkeley BioBusiness Association (B3A). My experience organizing medical conferences in medical school will help me contribute to Haas's student-run Business of Health Care conference. Leveraging my experience in setting up health clinics in the Amazon, I hope to recruit fellow Healthcare@Haas club members in leading a field trip to Brazil to study how to provide health-care consulting to remote regions. My long-time affiliation with Doctors without Borders will help me make substantive contributions to Haas's Challenge for Charity and Berkeley Solutions Group.

■ My contribution to my Columbia class will capitalize on my wide-ranging professional experiences in Australia's banking and mining industries as well as my California and Native American roots. But it will also be grounded in my willingness to always try the unknown in everything my classmates and I do together. Through the Hermes Society, for example, I can expand my personal boundaries by improving my ability to speak in front of groups. By serving as an ambassador for the MBA program, I can enhance potential applicants' understanding and appreciation of the program as Keisha Sullivan (Class of 2009) did for me. And through "The Bottom Line" I can build relationships with people outside the program and begin giving back immediately to the Columbia community.

Takeaways

- Diversity was not a "value-add" in this project—it was its heart. Had it not been for Francoise, Gustav, and Abdul, I would not have accomplished my objective. The management team expressed its appreciation for my work by offering me a full-time position as Mobile Star's global assignments manager. It was nice to be recognized, but the real winner was the diversity of my team.

- The world is shrinking; currencies, economies, and markets inexorably converge. Every individual and every society must discover its own way to celebrate this convergence while preserving—and celebrating—its own identity and uniqueness. At Purdue's Krannert School I will seek this perfect middle ground between unity and diversity in everything I do, in every life I touch.

- For me, culture shock—experiencing the foreign in sometimes jarring ways—is a natural part of doing business internationally. But "shock" does not need to be traumatic or unpleasant. Our São Paulo office served as a link between U.S. and Asian suppliers and Eastern European buyers, and these interactions—challenging as they could sometimes be—helped to hone my negotiation skills and my ability to sign large contracts. For all the differences between cultures, I've found that certain qualities, such as the ability to unify and motivate people, are shared by successful managers of any nationality.

- I offer to my HEC classmates my openness to new experiences, people, and cultures; my celebration of the ideal of "harmony" that music represents for me; and my willingness to work with them to make the HEC community a better place.

- I look forward to sharing the lessons I have learned from my own experience of diversity with my Stern classmates, who I am sure will help me further refine and reevaluate my view of what a truly global perspective is.

- I realize that Kellogg's familial team culture demands a tremendous contribution from each of its students, so the core value of my contribution at Kellogg will be this: if my own life can change so dramatically, then

I owe it to my Kellogg peers to share my message of faith in personal potential; openness to others, diversity, and change; and the joyful pursuit of personal passions.

- I look forward to sharing with my Chicago GSB classmates my courage to dream and my belief in the kind of integrity that remains true to traditional values and cultural heritage.

- Through my legal background; firsthand knowledge of the differences between the Russian, European, and U.S. markets; demonstrated skills in management and entrepreneurialism; and personal experience in cultural diversity and risk-taking, I can offer my Fuqua classmates an unusually rich perspective on both business and life.

- I believe that the language ability, personal touch, and cultural sensitiveness I demonstrated at HSBC prove the power of diversity as a business tool. But I needed to move to HSBC's diversity-embracing corporate culture to begin to wield that tool. I have chosen MIT Sloan's MBA program for precisely the same reason.

Part IV

Other Topics

Chapter 7 Perfect Phrases for Challenge and Defining Moment Essays

"Tell us about a time when you tried to reach a goal or complete a task that was challenging, difficult, or frustrating."

(Stanford)

"We all experience significant events or milestones that influence the course of our lives. Briefly describe such an event and how it affected you."

(USC Marshall)

Business schools believe they can find out a lot about how applicants will deal with the challenge of business school and a management career by seeing how they've dealt with the challenges they've encountered already. Moreover, applicants who can show they've come through a lot to get where they are today will be viewed with special favor by admissions readers who are happy to reward determination and focus. Making difficult decisions, overcoming obstacles, battling through resistance—all of these can make powerful material for challenge-type essays.

Defining moments do not necessarily need to have been challenges. But as intensely significant, even life-changing experiences that helped shape the person you are, they are close cousins of the challenge essay and often share a similar organization. The perfect phrases in this chapter are organized using our customary structure:

- Context
- What you did (your response to the challenge or your description of the defining moment)
- Result
- Takeaways

Context

- "I don't have to give you any damn report," Davis barked. I could not believe my ears. It had been just two weeks since my promotion to project lead for ScopeQuest, Yohimbe's latest network detection product, and I had been given only six months to ensure that a basic ScopeQuest was ready for 250 important customers. I was directly coordinating the efforts of seven developers—including Davis, six certification engineers, and one product release engineer—and discussed our progress with two vice presidents. I was exhilarated by this level of responsibility, but nothing prepared me for what I heard when I asked Davis for the weekly progress report. Older, technically competent, and indispensable to our team, Davis was also often argumentative, refused to provide required reports, and frequently mocked me for "wasting" my time preparing reports.

- "Oh my God, you were placed at Cherry Street!" My teacher-in-training classmates at Concordia University consoled me as word spread that my first trial by fire as a public school teacher would occur in one of the Twin Cities' least "comfortable and convenient" schools— Cherry Street High School in St. Paul's tough inner city. Soon, some of the details about Cherry Street began to emerge: a school administrator had been gunned down when his shady business dealings went awry; a child of one of the teachers assaulted someone with a deadly weapon.

- At Exxon Nigeria one of my major roles is to provide geophysical services to the operating business units. During one such project I presented my project manager with my meticulously processed geophysical seismic data only to discover that he was unhappy with my results. He had already received a contractor's results, which looked appealing to him but suspicious in its details to me. Since it is very hard to verify the correctness of seismic data processing results without actually drilling the well, my manager was siding with the contractor's rosy estimate and implicitly questioning my technical capability and competence.

- Near the end of my productive college class presidency a fellow student shot and killed his girlfriend in the school's library and later committed suicide. Nothing like this had ever happened before, and our conservative Baptist campus and the entire county were shaken to the core. When a teacher asked me what I wanted to do as president to help heal the shock and rebuild class spirit, I didn't know what to say.

- My wife Dawn had had morning sickness before, but this was something different. Early into her pregnancy, Dawn's symptoms worsened, so I had her move back to Atlanta where her parents could take better care of her and our two-year-old daughter, Aimee. When Dawn began repeatedly vomiting blood, however, I took an advance leave and immediately returned to Georgia. The test results showed high levels of thyroid hormones—harmless if caused by pregnancy, but if preexisting, potentially affecting both Dawn and our baby.

- The day I gave up the priesthood to pursue my passion for finance I felt both exhilaration and a deep sense of loss.

- Approximately 20 years ago, a young man walked into a boy's life and through his generosity and kindness helped change it forever. I am that boy, and if it were not for the influence and guidance of that man, Kijana Mbeki, I would not be here today.

- It's only 10 days into basic training, and our drill sergeant is telling us to retrieve our enlistment contracts from our wall lockers. We sit on the polished tiles and read for the first time the clause that says you can be reassigned "in time of war." Sergeant Olson then turns on the television, and grimly we watch scenes of warfare in Afghanistan. We have been reassigned to infantry training. Next stop: Operation Enduring Freedom.

- When I grew up, Taiwan was under martial law. All information was filtered through government censors before it reached the public. When I was in elementary and junior high school, I had completely bought into the government's propaganda; I was willing to stand up and defend Kuomintang, Taiwan's ruling party. One summer afternoon, I went into a small bookstore near my junior high school, waiting for the usual tropical rain to pass. Behind an obscured counter, I accidentally discovered a whole shelf of books marked "Prohibited by Government." I began to read.

- I experienced a defining moment during my junior year of high school. I was with a friend as we left my date's house after dropping her off on Halloween. Her neighbors, who were hosting a party for a local gang, recognized us as being from a rival neighborhood and proceeded to confront us. My friend made it to our car and hit one of the gang members as he sped away. I did not make it to the car. While I watched in disbelief as my friend drove off, one of the gang members reached for a gun.

What You Did

- Budget constraints required me to lead the audit while supervising a team of auditors from Ernst & Young's Paris and New York offices, and I had only four weeks to complete the audit report. This was a challenge because in Paris I had to lead E&Y auditors who were French CPAs with five more years' experience than me. By delegating astutely and taking advantage of the CPAs' strong accounting background, I was able to mesh our multifunctional, multicultural talents efficiently and diplomatically, and we completed the Paris portion of the audit a week earlier than expected.

- To persuade Silver Lake's partners, I first retained an IT consulting service and performed rigorous due diligence with it and a potential coinvestor on PerfectTen's technology. After affirming its uniqueness, I read extensively on the industry and wrote an investment memorandum detailing the company's market potential.

I then performed a valuation analysis for similar public companies and concluded that PerfectTen's equity was reasonably priced. Marshaling my evidence, I formally recommended that the partners invest. Because of my high rankings as a research analyst, they listened but remained skeptical despite my strong supporting data. So I scheduled another meeting where I offered additional research from industry experts and held a conference call with a Forrester Research analyst. That finally convinced two of the partners, and a day later the most senior partner left me an exhilarating voice message agreeing to make the deal.

- Though the students were disciplined when Ms. Rainier was in the room, when I first took over, they got rowdy, complaining, "Why do we have to learn this?" I realized right away that at Cherry Street respect did not come automatically; it had to be earned. I began earning it by first sharing my own story. I told them how, as a high school student, mathematics had benefited me by enabling me to score well enough on the SAT to earn academic scholarships for college. I helped them identify with me by telling them how I had had to pay for my entire education. Gradually, they began to see me as a role model for the success they could achieve. Then, after establishing rapport, something strange and unexpected occurred: We actually began to have fun! I did have to send the occasional student to detention, but most were eager to learn. When I stayed late to help the Advanced Placement students prepare for the exam, the entire class showed up. Little did I know that this would become a daily event for us.

- Traveling to Manila, I met my 20 green developers and assessed their skill levels and personalities. Clearly, mentoring them would be my next difficult challenge. Because they obviously lacked advanced Java knowledge, I arranged on-project training, but I decided to teach them about the project's relevant fashion retail topics through my own presentations. I soon discovered, however, that the developers viewed me as the pricing system's "guru"—the only one capable of understanding it—so I had to first remove the esoteric aura surrounding the pricing system. Patiently, I answered all their questions until they saw me as teacher, mentor, and friend, but *not* as unapproachable guru. To promote teamwork, I also took the whole team out for tasty pancit palabok at Jollibee's (on their recommendation). This gave me the chance to find out who was compatible with whom, which helped me assign the groups for each module.

- The only solution was joining forces. I called our first group meeting and said, "This is a pilot program: we have a great opportunity to show the entire company how Verizon can sell one solution." We immediately began exchanging leads and contacts and then began going on sales calls together. We practically refused to sell one component without including another business unit's component.

■ I asked doctors in the unit how they could deal with such intense, emotionally wrenching moments. Several replied that they detached themselves emotionally; others said that it was just "part of the job." I was uncomfortable with the idea of becoming so diminished in sensitivity toward human suffering. Continuing to gain clinical exposure as a volunteer at the Portland University Medical Center, I encountered similar situations that reinforced how emotionally difficult providing critical care can be. I discussed my hesitancy about dealing with the realities of death and human suffering with a premed advisor, Dr. Wu, at Portland University. Ultimately, she helped me accept that I did not possess the unique attitude toward human suffering that is required of surgeons and critical care doctors.

■ After a preliminary analysis, I decided to commit my life savings of $150,000 to founding a company to build the structure, since I lacked the resources to develop it myself. All I needed was the owner's commitment to invest $1.5 million. I delved into a meticulous feasibility analysis, which demonstrated that the development would realize the owner a 55 percent return. I made a thorough presentation to the owner, underscoring the higher profit potential of an apartment building, recommending a reputable architect, and assuring him that my company would be staffed with industry veterans. When he still held back, I threw in a $2,000 daily late penalty. After I assembled my team, work began.

- I picked up one of the books marked "Prohibited by Government" and began to read how the Kuomintang had controlled the media and military so as to smother the development of Taiwanese democracy. It was an intellectually liberating experience that gradually dismantled my blind faith in Kuomintang's policy and leaders. I dug deeper and investigated the so-called White Terror—the name the government's critics gave to the secret police's censorship tactics. In the memoirs and historical photo collections I leafed through, page after page recorded the blood and pain of the people who had given their lives to guarantee the civil rights of everyone on the beautiful island of Formosa.

- I went back to check my geophysical data to see whether they were flawed in any way, but I had done everything correctly. If I told my manager my geophysical report was the best I could provide, he would choose the contractor's rosier results and conclude that I was technically incompetent. If I tried other techniques to "improve" the final report, he would object that I had spent too much time on the project,

➡

which would confirm his doubts about my abilities. Since I was confident in my competence and my analysis, I decided that the best way to convince my manager was to simulate the contractor's processing. By making some easily disprovable scientific assumptions and layering cosmetic processing techniques over my results, I too generated appealing results. I showed the two sets of results to my manager and said: "One is the honest processing; the other is not done in a theoretically rigorous way. Which one do you like?"

■ That evening the planning team reconvened to salvage the exercise. We broke into groups to work out the small problems first. My expertise was in airborne submarine defense, so I spent the next two hours going over check-in procedures, aerial tactics, and ship-to-air coordination with my Malaysian counterparts. They were familiar with these procedures, but working in a second language can make even simple radio communications difficult. Even with my experience, it is sometimes hard for me to keep track of all the radio chatter in and out of an aircraft in a battle group environment. After smoothing out the fine details, we brought the groups back together to go over any outstanding questions. The long day turned into a late night as we reviewed the causes of the problems and developed and distributed solutions.

Result

- With our differences resolved and our working relationship intact, Antonio and I went on to nail down the design of *our* solution and divide the development tasks between us. In mid–2006, we successfully released the product, which has generated annual revenues of $2 million for JoyToy and entertains more than 60,000 users worldwide. Meanwhile, I have developed a close relationship with Antonio. I have helped him improve his spoken English skills through our frequent phone conversations, for example, and three months after signing off on the joint effort, I received a call from a thrilled Antonio announcing the birth of his son.

- Luckily, my strategy of combining theoretical knowledge with my area of special interest earned a 78 percent return over the three-month period, outperforming my nearest competitor by at least 20 percent.

- Presented with these and other benefits, this time they agreed to my computerization proposal. When my accounting system came online five months later, it eliminated many potentially costly logistical errors and the need to hire a full-time bookkeeper (at $45,000 a year).

- To this day, I am not sure how I moved so quickly through the ranks of the Young Native American

Professional Association's Washington, D.C., chapter. In only three-plus years, I went from social chair to national liaison for the local chapter. This past September, I was elected community relations director of YNAPA's parent organization, Young Native Americans United (YNAU), a 24-chapter organization whose current membership exceeds 40,000. As the community relations director, my role is to help young Native Americans get educations and competitive jobs and increase public perception of young Native Americans as a productive force in all aspects of American life. As a member of the eight-person executive board of YNAU, I am helping the organization expand nationally, spreading the word about our 501(c)3 charitable foundation, and soliciting corporate sponsorship for our scholarship fund for college-age Native Americans.

- I delivered the first module, which could have taken us a year to develop by ourselves, in approximately six months. Not only did SorcerySoft maintain its credibility, but it also enjoyed a 10 percent ($3 million) increase in revenues as customers began lining up for the impending releases. In the bargain, SorcerySoft also found a long-term partner. Impressed by my work, management has since entrusted me with the responsibility of managing our existing FutureTrek product as its technical lead.

- Change came slowly, but persistence and the effective management and motivation of people made the difference. After weeks away from my family in a politically unstable environment where machine-gun-toting soldiers were a common sight, I watched the first flight for Heart airport lift off without incident on May 19, 2006. Today, SkyAfghan has a branch office in Kandahar and is the fastest-growing airline in the country. It was a supreme test of my managerial skills and creativity, and I'm proud to have met the challenge.

- We soon transformed ourselves from five "lions" into a tight pack of wolves driven to prove that Cox's "One Solution" truly works. Within a year, our sales had rocketed from zero to $200 million, and we were invited to meet with CEO Jim Robbins.

- Within nine months, we were receiving increased coverage from industry publications and had grown revenues from strategic partner channels by 150 percent, setting the stage for our acquisition by industry leader Diversified China Holdings in 2003.

Takeaways

- I had naively believed that decisions involving the environment were primarily driven by facts and not political considerations. I quickly learned that in contrast to the predictable world of engineering science, even solutions with a clear quantitative and logical basis can be sacrificed in favor of short-term political benefits. Reevaluating my faith in the effectiveness of rational decision making was not easy. But today I understand how to take political influences into account when making fact-driven decisions.

- The challenge and controversy of the IRS audit was truly a "crucible" experience for me because it was the first time I had ever been challenged every step of the way. The audit reinforced my conviction that objective evidence cannot be refuted—and should not be backed away from. It also affirmed that, no matter how bad the odds may sometimes look, two parties can come to agreement once they truly understand all the issues.

- Although Angel Partners has not yet succeeded financially, it has helped me learn what success and consequently failure really mean to me. There is no failure worse than letting down people who put trust in your leadership. Every growth plan I develop in the future will contain a detailed contingency plan that will allow me to minimize, if not eliminate, the need to downsize. I have learned that success is not only about the success of a product or financial gain; it must also include the success of every contributor.

■ This experience taught me that anyone and everyone can suffer from discrimination, despite the laws prohibiting it. I am particularly sensitive now to the stereotypes women face in the oceanic sciences. In college, I noticed that in engineering courses women team members were usually assigned the least technically challenging tasks, for example, literature searches instead of actual design. So in my own senior project, I made sure that was not the case by dividing the work fairly so everyone was challenged. Professionally, I continue my awareness of discrimination and work to ensure that each of the three women on my Deepwater Sciences team can contribute fully to the team.

■ In retrospect, my decision to move to the agency side was the most important single decision of my career. It rounded out my skill set, broadened my experience base, and gave me a new, wider perspective on my career and myself. I learned the ins and outs of agency life and media strategy for business-to-business clients, and I escaped the pigeonhole of sales, opening up a whole new career avenue. After nearly a year at Rasmussen Group as a media planner, in fact, I felt comfortable enough to reach for experience at a higher level, manage large projects, and work more directly with clients on their "big-picture" plans. By knowing myself, examining my options, and having the courage to make a change, I made the right decision.

■ Svetlana's illness has reminded me of what I really care about. We are resolved to love and care for our new child, normal or not, and our lives will probably never be the same. Wherever my career leads me, the most important consideration now will always be the needs and wishes of my family, and my gratitude for and enjoyment of family and life will be greater than ever before.

■ I will never regret becoming a priest. It exposed me to leadership opportunities most 19-year-olds never face. It also gave me the chance to discover what I really wanted by exploring the alternatives. Deciding to leave the priesthood meant abandoning a life and a definition of myself that had great meaning for me. But because of the sense of challenge and excitement I feel every morning and the positive good my career has made possible, I can honestly say it was a decision I have never regretted making.

■ The impact of this period on my life was both subtle and total. Although my values are the same, I now have a much deeper confidence in my instincts. I know I can adapt to new challenges and learn unfamiliar topics quickly. And though living overseas has given me a greater appreciation for being American, I now see myself as a "permanent" citizen of the most mysterious and exciting city in the world.

■ Surviving that training course was a rite of passage, a journey into the deepest part of me. I overcame my fears and doubts and guided a squad of men shaken by suicides and an unforeseen war into becoming more than they had known how to be before. Beginning my "defining moment" as a 19-year-old boy surrounded by strangers, I emerged from it leading men who had become my brothers.

■ As my plane descended into John Wayne Airport, I had already won. My decision to embrace change optimistically made it possible for me to land my first job within days of arriving, which set the stage for my next move up, to Pacific Life, a year later. Three months after arriving in Orange County I sold the return portion of my round-trip ticket back home. There was no point in keeping it. My new life in America was well underway, and the last thing I needed was a security blanket.

■ Whenever I recall that morning in Fallujah, I sit up straight and thank God for getting me out of there. I also thank the bus driver who mustered up enough courage to drive past the mob. Surprisingly, he was from the same tribe as the rioters and didn't support the imposition of Shiite rule any more than they did. Unlike them, however, he chose to protect us even at risk to his own life. The bridge he built that day saved our lives and reinforced my belief that, in spite of cultural and geographical distances, we still share the common bonds of humanity.

- Far from "wasting my talent," my decision to enter private industry has enabled me to pursue my scientific work in a more pragmatic way while fulfilling my desire to work for the greatest possible public benefit. It has tested and strengthened my scientific abilities and unleashed my intellectual and managerial creativity. If I had not "examined" the false assumptions that lie behind the stigma some academics still attach to private industry, I might not be in a position to help lead the exciting changes about to take place in oncology and the treatment of human disease.

Chapter 8 Perfect Phrases for Failure and Ethics Essays

"Describe a failure or setback that you have experienced. What role did you play and what did you learn about yourself?"

(Wharton)

"Describe an ethical dilemma that you faced in your professional career. How was it resolved and what did you learn from the experience?"

(Indiana)

Business schools ask applicants about failures for several reasons. First, failures are often opportunities for growth. Admissions officers want to know whether you are an evolving person capable of learning, adjusting to setbacks, and maturing. Second, *what* you fail at (and what failures you choose to write about) says something about what matters to you and what kinds of risks you're willing to take to achieve your goals. Third, how you approach this question enables admissions committees to gauge your personality as well as the veracity of your application: applicants who try to weasel out of admitting a real

173

failure lose credibility in the committee's eyes, as do applicants whose failures are trivial or overly common.

Essays about ethical situations enable business schools to evaluate your ability to analyze the difficult moral choices that all managers occasionally confront. The story you choose to tell in this essay and the reasons you give for making the ethical choices you did tell admissions committees a lot about your values and your mind. The best stories are not about bribes being rejected, but tough-call dilemmas where none of the solutions looks particularly appealing.

This chapter's perfect phrases for failure and ethics-related essays are organized as follows:

- Failure: context
- Failure: analysis
- Failure: takeaways
- Ethics: context
- Ethics: analysis
- Ethics: what you did (your ethical decision)
- Ethics: takeaways

Failure: Context

- "We made it. It's a done deal." A palpable sense of relief ran through Sierra Land Holding's business development office when Abbeville Homes' lawyers finally approved a $400 million deal for our Sunnyton development site. After three months of intense negotiations, we had an agreement partially vindicating our public vow to complete two deals in 2005 and assuring us of investments in our two subsequent developments. Then a week later the ax fell. Abbeville backed out of the agreement because of doubts raised by environmental agency decisions. Thousands of hours of work suddenly evaporated.

- How bad was it? It was so bad I could see the looks of empathy in my colleagues' eyes. As they squirmed in their seats eagerly awaiting the end of my agonizing two-hour presentation, I could see they were actually feeling for me. It was so bad that afterwards Ananth, my usually respectful partner in our Chartered Financial Analyst (CFA) course for BankBoston's in-house learning program, could only say, "Wow, what were you doing?" My failure last year while delivering my half of a four-hour CFA prep course to the New Haven analysts' group taught me a crucial lesson about preparation and time management that I will never forget.

- The moment remains so vivid: the flawed report, the CFO's office, the flight home, and the weeks of soul-searching that followed. The day I left Milan Investment Partners I had to face the fact that I had failed to meet strongly set personal objectives. I felt an emptiness I had never known before.

- Nothing could have been worse than the humiliation I felt as I listened to the university's president chide me for my willful disregard of the university's honor code— unless it was seeing the look in my father's deeply disappointed eyes, hearing my mother lapse into tears, and trying to explain to a younger brother who idolized me why I had let my friends use my PC to hack into the registrar's office mainframe.

- I was failing at Bank of America because, fresh from school, I had made money the primary criterion in my postcollege placement plan. I was failing to adjust to the company's culture because I had not tried to find out what it was. I had made a serious career misstep and was miserable.

- I regard this as a failure because I had spent my college career believing in the Greek system and in my Gamma Gamma brothers. As I learned what it meant to be ostracized in your own organization and to see best friends suddenly showing overt hostility, I began to question my decision to be part of that system.

- Flying to Mexico City in October 2005 to contain the situation, I felt a deep sense of disappointment in myself. I had failed to envision the problems that arise when an organization tries to expand rapidly. I had also betrayed the trust my family placed in me by failing to do the due diligence that would have been my first priority in my day job.

Failure: Analysis

- Why did I fail? The Shimonoseki experience taught me an important strategy for coping with politically charged environments: join forces. Too late I realized that by working with the other antiwhaling initiatives we might have had more success in convincing the Japanese authorities to halt the expedition.

- If I had known more about new-product development, venture capital, and entrepreneurship, my presentation could have been much more convincing and LifeRenewal's management might have decided to fund my breakthrough. Moreover, I realize now that I could also have left LifeRenewal and tried to sell my idea to a biotech firm or VC company or obtained small business grants from research funds. Instead, I put my research on the shelf and moved on.

- Though I had assertively communicated my concerns to Tony, I had not presented any facts, such as the percentage of projects that fail because of a lack of appropriate knowledge-transfer exercises, that might have convinced him. If I had presented my concerns more effectively during the weekly meeting with the Hewlett-Packard client manager, I could have created a debate between HP and PricewaterhouseCoopers, forcing a joint decision.

- I knew immediately what was wrong. By focusing on producing a competitive plan, I had become blind to an inherent flaw: we had to commit a substantial up-front investment with no guarantee of completion. Rather than seek the advice of experienced experts, I had allowed myself to become spellbound by research and case studies.

- I failed, first, because the attractiveness of CB Richard Ellis's fundamentals, its leadership position, and the value the Mekong City proposal created led me to make an incorrect estimate of the premium foreign investors would pay to enter the Vietnamese market. Second, I failed because I overestimated the willingness of Vietnam's own strategic buyers to invest in Mekong City as well as the likelihood that the national assembly would pass legislation allowing foreign ownership of real estate companies. I did not appreciate the unpredictability of the legislative process and the influence that Vinaconex, Vietnam's largest construction company, would have in delaying the legislation. Today, the legislation still has not passed, and because of the lack of foreign and local buyers, we have a stake in Mekong City we are unable to sell.

- Could I have averted this pointless loss? Although I was confident of my data, I failed to vigorously defend my position and shied away from confrontation. Instead of marshaling all my data and persuasive abilities to modify my manager's flawed approach, I gave in to his seniority and demonstrated loyalty to him rather than to the company itself.

- General Motors had only asked us to tell it which plants to close, but I had let my sympathy for my friends at the suburban Memphis plant convince me to step beyond my professional responsibility and provide an unrequested alternative proposal.

Failure: Takeaways

- While making mistakes is unavoidable, and even necessary to one's learning curve, repeating them definitely is not. I have learned to ask all essential questions ahead of time to avoid similar failures, regardless of whom such questions may make uncomfortable.

- The failure of the Rapid City project taught me that it is important to firm up business requirements early so no drastic changes are made to them later unless absolutely necessary. I learned from colleagues in Newark that their business requirements also underwent rounds and rounds of revision, often with little value added. I learned a lesson I'm sure I'll apply repeatedly in my career: If a team dwells too much on one aspect of a project, it may lose sight of the bigger picture. I also learned that in a partnership it is critical for partners to be open to each other so they can readily understand each other's difficulties. Without communication, problems can only snowball.

- I discovered the hard way that establishing a new business demands a serious commitment—interest, part-time hours, and start-up cash alone won't make a business sustainable. I also learned that friendship among the principals of a business won't help it survive in the absence of a shared vision and shared responsibility.

- This experience taught me a very painful leadership lesson: in any situation it is vitally important to identify the stakeholders and then understand their emotions and motivations, especially when a project's success depends on their support. Ultimately, I learned that

I could have been much more effective as a leader if I had taken the project team members' concerns into account earlier and involved them more aggressively in the WiMax project from the beginning.

- This setback made me a bolder entrepreneur and better leader. I learned that I must aggressively commit 100 percent from day one if I want a venture to succeed. I realized that as a leader I am more than a manager—my presence is as valuable as my analysis and strategy formulation. I also learned never to hire close compatriots, no matter how competent they are.

- The most important lesson I learned from this unhappy experience is the price that must be paid for mediocrity.

- This episode taught me that when you make a private equity investment, it is imperative that you have a clear exit strategy and make conservative risk management assumptions or your investment may stay tied up indefinitely.

- SailSure's collapse forced me to realize that there are two key factors to the success of a business: developing long-term business partnerships and building supportive networks with international managers. This setback taught me that a viable business requires more than competent managers and good products. It also needs a global network of influential contacts.

- Evaluating the experience later, I realized that it is perfectly reasonable for a business to pursue short-term goals that are radically different from its long-term ones, if, as in our case, they ultimately finance the company's core business.

- I have learned to bring visibility to my findings by creating forums for constructive debate. I have discovered how to creatively and tenaciously build positions of strength that will enable me to go around obstacles that threaten the well-being of the corporation.

Ethics: Context

- Just one month into my new assignment I started to notice inconsistencies between the product performance data I saw and the data Derek reported to Value Shop. Derek convinced me that I was reviewing old data and told me to stay focused on developing the marketing plan. My workload was huge, so I gradually forgot about the inconsistencies. The more I got to know my undeniably brilliant manager, however, the more I noticed how he manipulated information to please his audience. When I spoke to him about it, he told me that as you grow in the company, you sometimes have to stretch the truth to sell proposals. This made me uncomfortable, but I let it drop. Then, two months before the launch, with production underway, I saw him stretch data to obtain management approval on advertising claims. Worse, these data were being forwarded to a government agency for final advertising approval.

- During my second year at Potomac Partners, a senior consultant I was working with asked me to give him confidential information about a small software company whose business plan I had just assessed. Of course, I immediately reminded him that I was not authorized to disclose any information. The next day, however, I surprised him as he searched my shelves for the files. I was stunned. Should I continue working for a colleague who had gone against my ethics and express wishes, not to mention the policies of the firm?

- WiSys's account manager at Southeastern Federal (SF) called an urgent meeting and revealed that thanks to an accounting glitch, we were behind quarterly revenue targets by a whopping $6 million. He told us that we needed to do whatever we could to "stretch" the project estimates we gave SF. Because I had five projects in the pipeline, all in proposal-estimate stage, Minglie conveyed his "expectations" very pointedly to me.

- The role Kristine described sounded great until she told me the client would be informed I was an "expert" in ATM systems. I had a good technology background but

➡

not in the electronic funds industry or its transaction systems.

- Within six months we had grown to eight employees, but the economic downturn forced me to begin planning a scale-down of my operations. I would have to let people go. Of the seven employees my books told me to lay off, however, two were a married couple. The husband was seriously ill; his wife couldn't work because she had to stay home and care for him. Unemployment benefits would not be enough to keep them afloat.

- As I read the project prospectus, I noticed the glaring omission of the expensive gas-scrubbing equipment OSHA requires for all U.S. tests. Clearly, Enerplex was trying to take advantage of Guatemala's weak air-quality standards. Without such gas-scrubbing equipment our Guatemalan workers would be exposed to carcinogenic toxins like benzene and dioxins.

- As First Union's recruiting season was winding down Bill, one of my managers, asked me to follow up with a potential "star recruit" who was deciding whether to accept an outstanding offer. Upon calling her, I learned that the recruit, Ann, was leaning toward accepting our offer because Bill had promised her that she would be able to work exclusively in our investment banking group. I hesitated before telling Ann that I would get back to her on that, fully knowing that she would not be able to join investment banking because it was a really small unit that had just hired all the staff it could accommodate. Furthermore, Bill was not even from the investment banking group but from commercial lending. When I told Bill about the situation, he explained that I needed to get the recruit to accept the offer at all costs because our First Bank of Florida engagement required someone with her experience in real estate loans. He ordered me to try to convince Ann that the investment banking department invited staff transfers from commercial lending.

- During Pacific Northwest Trust's long attempt to acquire Nuvatrix, a major biotech firm in Silicon Valley, I worked closely with "Paul," Nuvatrix's assistant treasurer, over eight months. One morning after a working session, he asked me if local newspaper reports were true that Pacific Northwest was planning to lay off his company's employees as part of our takeover plan. Since I hadn't seen the report, I did not answer him on the spot, but his question put me in a difficult situation. Pacific Northwest was in fact seriously evaluating a contingent layoff plan.

- Only four days before the client's workshop with venture capitalists, the CFO asked me to make a small but significant change to the business model he had fully approved only the day before. In creating the model, I had determined a realistic market penetration rate for the start-up's business based on several key elements, including the expected growth in the virtualization software market and our client's capabilities. However, the CFO was now requesting that I change the market penetration rate to a higher percentage, thereby inflating the client's projected revenues and increasing the business model's attractiveness to the venture capitalists.

Ethics: Analysis

- Confronting Steve did not work, and given his managers' regard for him, going above him could ruin my career.

- My dilemma was that I was working for two clients, the homeowners' association and Bowling Green Group. It challenged my professional values to expose one of my clients, but I could not simply ignore unethical practices.

- Though an overestimate of a few hundred dollars would pass unnoticed and enable Vosotron to meet its targets, Alim's strategy seemed unscrupulous to me. I see these clients every day; we share personal stories, and we trust each other implicitly. And it was precisely this trust that Alim wanted me to exploit. If I disobeyed him, I could lose my job; if I overestimated, I would be disloyal to my clients.

- On my way back to Seattle, I struggled with how to respond to Paul, since my personal instinct to be truthful contradicted my loyalty to Pacific Northwest Trust's interests. Worse, over the past eight months, Paul and I had developed a good working relationship and even friendship. By asking me whether Pacific Northwest intended to downsize Nuvatrix after our acquisition, he was clearly demonstrating his trust in me. But I also felt just as strongly that, as a Pacific Northwest employee, I needed to guard the confidentiality of our takeover plan.

- I had a clear impression that Mark lacked the sales abilities that are critical to performing well as an insurance broker. Also, I felt his heart was not really in life insurance. However, I knew that my frank opinion could put his job and career at Allstate in jeopardy at a moment when he needed the job more than ever, because his wife had just lost hers.

- In an instant, I knew exactly how the choices before me would play out. If I just ignored my mistake, I would get my security badge, be on my way into the vault, and begin working. There was no way they would ask me to present a U.S. passport or birth certificate. However, if

I truthfully pointed out that my badge mistakenly identified me as a U.S. citizen, not only would they ask to see my green card, but, worse, my own negligence would be exposed: in all my excitement about seeing Fort Knox I had completely forgotten that I needed to bring my green card to enter a federal facility! Besides the personal embarrassment, our team would be short one auditor for at least a day, I would have to trouble a friend to mail the card down, and I'd perhaps be seen as unprofessional by Firstar's management.

Ethics: What You Did (Your Ethical Decision)

- After carefully weighing my dilemma, I decided to uphold confidentiality while still addressing Paul's fears. I discussed my solution with my team principal, and he agreed with my plan.

- Examining my options, I decided that I simply could not accept the idea of releasing a substandard product.

- Deciding I could not justify misrepresenting my background and capability, I declined the ATM project three days after Kristine's offer. She asked me to rethink my decision, but I was firm.

- The colleagues and family members I asked for help gave conflicting advice, so ultimately, I went with my gut and decided my manager had to be told. The only way I could think of to do that without getting Nigel in trouble was to share the blame for the mistake. I knew I could get by with a mistake because I'd just received an outstanding performance evaluation and my manager respected my work. As long as he thought we were both culpable, he would be less likely to punish Nigel.

- But under the pressure of the situation and having no time to reflect, I instinctively answered my supervisor honestly, telling him that, despite Mark's proven knowledge of insurance products, he lacked the basic skills to succeed as a salesman. I then stressed his other capabilities and suggested he be relocated to a different area. When I left, I was confident my supervisor would do his best to help Mark stay with Allstate.

- After much thought, I decided that I had the right to decline working for Lincoln but that I also had a professional responsibility to the firm to complete my current project with him. Moreover, I was not personally prepared to create a crisis that might eventually harm my own interests. Three months later, however, when I was asked to join Lincoln on one of his teams, I gracefully declined. The "borrowed file" incident had destroyed my confidence in a colleague and a bit of my own naïveté, but it gave me valuable insight into the realities of business ethics.

- After hours of deliberation, I decided that rejecting the assignment on moral grounds would not help the Guatemalan workers who faced exposure—someone else would just take the job. I therefore informed my manager that I would accept the assignment only if he would also nominate me as the safety officer of the pilot experiment. Later, I persuaded him to allocate a modest budget for protective organic vapor masks, and while in Guatemala I trained the local workers in their use and explained the dangers of prolonged exposure.

Ethics: Takeaways

- Sometimes standing by your beliefs is not only personally satisfying; it's the best *business* decision.

- Because of that experience, I learned how to systematically communicate our integrity requirements to prospective investors and to verify their track records before establishing serious contacts.

- I personally believe these seemingly insignificant "no-one-will-know" ethical situations are the most important in life. While the immediate consequences may seem harmless, when a person gets used to compromising in noncritical situations, there is ultimately a cumulative effect that affects the way he or she faces the tougher ethical quandaries.

■ This project shocked me into acknowledging that a small company can have the power to affect the actions of even the biggest global corporations. It also sharpened my negotiation skills by giving me the chance to serve as a broker in resolving an important issue between two longtime partners. Furthermore, I learned how to stick to my ethical principles when confronting executives willing to do anything for personal profit.

Chapter 9 Perfect Phrases for Social Impact and Change Essays

"USC has garnered national acclaim for its emphasis on community outreach and service. How have you impacted your community?"

(USC Marshall)

"In discussing Columbia Business School, Dean R. Glenn Hubbard remarked, 'We have established the mind-set that entrepreneurship is about everything you do.' Please discuss a time in your own life when you have identified and captured an opportunity."

(Columbia)

D o you have a heart? Is there room in your life for something besides self and career? Essay topics on community and social impact topics help admissions committees answer these questions. Social entrepreneurship, sustainable development, and corporate social responsibility are more than just buzzwords. They're core components of many B-schools' curricula today. To show your well-roundedness and concern for larger issues, it's often effective to devote one of your essays to your community involvements, even though only a few schools have explicit social impact topics. Likewise, only a few schools have explicit change, innovation, or entrepreneurship essay topics, but they too can be potentially powerful topics, especially if you have a track record of innovation or entrepreneurial goals. This chapter's perfect social impact and change phrases are organized as follows:

- Social impact: context
- Social impact: what you did
- Social impact: takeaways
- Change: what you did (your innovation or change)
- Change: takeaways

Social Impact: Context

- Mobile Heights and East Mobile might as well be on different planets. Mobile Heights boasts wealth and historic mansions, while East Mobile has potholed streets and steel-barred storefronts. Police cars are as common in East Mobile as BMWs are in Palo Alto. Yet East Mobile was home to fourteen teenagers I was determined to convince should go to college. Growing up to succeed was not really a choice for me. My parents sent me to the best schools and best summer camps, and encouraged me to dream my most ambitious dreams. But I believe that anyone who is really given the chance can succeed.

- I could see the fear of death in the eyes of the animals gathered at the local temple. Some had even started screaming. As the traditional ceremony came to an end, each of the goats and the sheep were sacrificed. Then the buffalo was dragged to the altar and tied mercilessly with a rope to the iron pillars. The chief landlord swung the sword like an instrument through the neck of the animal. To my horror the head of the animal was not completely severed and blood flowed everywhere. I had to do something about such cruelty.

- My identification with the mission of the Romanian Venture Business Women's Association—to promote entrepreneurial opportunities for women—began in my childhood, when as the daughter of a traditional Romanian family, I too was encouraged to surrender to a quiet, invisible role in society, quite unlike my brothers.

- I tried to picture little Adofo engulfed in the heat and hazard of a blacksmith's shop and didn't like the image. I was on my yearly visit to my hometown of Sironko, and Fabayo, my mother's domestic helper, had just mentioned she was sending her eight-year-old son to work for a blacksmith. I was appalled. Always struggling on their $400 annual income, she and her husband, a carpenter, had already pulled four of their children out of school so they could learn trades to support themselves. Now Adofo was to be the fifth. Since Fabayo and her husband's parents had done the same to them, they simply had no idea that staying in school might earn their children even better livelihoods as adults.

- Hearing is something young people take for granted. In my quest to be a professional drummer and singer, developing a hearing condition was the furthest thing from my mind. Unfortunately, in practicing and performing for a career in music, I was exposed to noise louder than the human auditory system was meant to take, and I developed hyperacusis, defined as a painful sensitivity to normal environmental sounds.

- In the spring of 1999, my younger sister QiaoQiao was diagnosed with a rare case of skin cancer and given three to six months to live. I believed—I knew—she would survive. In the meantime, she was spending her time in the hospital, missing school, and becoming morbidly preoccupied with her illness. I decided to tutor her in math and English. Soon, some of my friends started volunteering to help entertain QiaoQiao too. Gathering informally a few times a week, we quickly befriended other kids in the ward and began entertaining them with books, videogames, and comics.

▪ If it weren't for the volunteers of the Middle Eastern Students Association (MESA) at the University of Pennsylvania, my transition to U.S. life as a foreign student would have been far more unnerving. These generous people arranged a place for me to stay and helped me acclimate myself to a new educational system and social environment. I felt I owed them something.

Social Impact: What You Did

▪ At Swarthmore I was one of the core leaders of College Home Run, in which six of my Garnet baseball teammates and I used our "prestige" to get teenagers from Philadelphia interested in college.

▪ Because the school in Sironko could not teach the community's children for free and most poor families could not afford the tuition, in September 2005 I decided to organize free elementary education classes for kids like Adofo.

▪ At Texas Tech, I truly tried to involve myself in a variety of community-service initiatives. For example, I led six students in organizing events that raised $5,000 for The Safe Place, a nonprofit organization that provides shelter and support for runaway teens. I also cofounded Tech's Pet Fanciers Club, which through its 78 members sponsored dog and cat shows in the Lubbock area and

➡

tutored inner-city high school students. In my senior year, as a dorm advisor, I created a "social impact" theme on my floor of 30 residents through which we organized trips to food banks, elementary schools, and nursing homes. Finally, as an intern for U.S. Congressman Randy Neugebauer, I helped handle social-work cases involving worker's comp, food stamps, and unemployment training.

- As part of Pro Bono Consultants (PBC), I work with other business professionals to develop marketing and strategic plans for nonprofit agencies in New Orleans. PBC works as a nonprofit consulting service, enlisting a broad range of talented professionals from around the city to provide a useful community service while giving volunteers an opportunity to network and develop career skills. PBC has enabled me to find a personal, unique way to give back to the community that raised me, to develop as a consultant, and to network with a talented group of students and community leaders.

- I volunteered to coach handicapped individuals to compete in swimming for the Special Olympics at a YMCA in Vancouver, British Columbia. Every week I spent an hour with 12 adults, teaching them basic stroke techniques. As a young child, I had learned to swim at the same YMCA and discovered only later the key role that volunteers played in sustaining the program's success. Moreover, my Vancouver neighborhood offered painfully few services and activities for the handicapped, so I knew my contribution made a big difference.

- I spent three weeks of the summer of my freshman year in the remote rural village of Kundha Kulam working for Tata College Farm Corps, a student-led movement that provided free labor to India's economically challenged farming communities. After plowing the fields by day, we would listen to farmers' hardships at night. During the school year, we organized campus fairs so the farmers could sell directly to consumers, and I shared what I learned in an article for the school newspaper and during student marches.

- I'm particularly proud of the policy change I implemented last year in the Dover Free Clinic's treatment of strep throat. This disease can cause a sore throat in children, but more importantly it can also cause heart damage. Treating it effectively and quickly is critical. While the previous clinic policy, drug treatment, was effective, the drug's high cost meant we could rarely get enough donations from pharmaceutical companies to serve our population. I researched the medical literature and consulted with infectious disease specialists and local epidemiologists as well as the state public health department. Armed with my findings, I convinced the clinic to change the protocol from the expensive drug to a much cheaper but equally efficacious one that was available in a generic form and that pharmaceutical companies were much happier to donate in larger quantities.

- My gratitude is why I developed the University Scholarship Program at Dow Chemical. I convinced the company to subsidize 10 scholarships for students, like me, who had to work to pay for their college education. The candidates who qualify are those who have the skill set to work at Dow and are involved in charitable activities. I'm proud to say this program is now over six years old.

- In cooperation with our partner NGOs, Somalia Relief Corps has recently painted blackened walls and replaced faucets, showers, toilets, boilers, and washing machines throughout Mogadishu. Hundreds of meters of electrical cables have been installed, and neglected sewage and water pipes are now being repaired. Next, my 60 associates and I will begin fixing leaking roofs, adding new eaves, and, not least, constructing a playground for children.

- With Kaiwen's help, I convinced the entire office to participate in Society Day, a worldwide initiative in which all Lenovo employees dedicate one day to social work. For Society Day 2006, we refurbished a low-income school in Ping Yao. We recruited and motivated 162 practitioners to work united toward one beneficial goal: making the school a better place for its 678 students. To our enormous gratification our project won the Lenovo 2006 Best Global Impact Day award, which included a $25,000 prize. After a year of amazing progress, our enlarged Impact Program team won the Lenovo 2007 Best Global Impact Program award, which included $50,000 dollars to continue our community work. Moreover, LLP—a government regulatory institution that's Shanxi province's center for philanthropy—recognized Lenovo Taiyuan as a "socially responsible enterprise," which opened up many potential client network opportunities.

Social Impact: Takeaways

- The feeling of gratification I gained from knowing I had been able to help three young lives find health and happiness is impossible for me to express.
- I have not yet realized my dream of completely breaking the cycle of illiteracy, but I have sowed the seeds of transformation.
- Seeing the determined faces of these children has helped me to understand the concept of teamwork in new ways. Disabled, I have learned, does not mean "unabled"—their ability to work together as a team is as natural and sincere as any "normal" group of people I have met.

➡

- The sudden awareness of my privilege simply to be healthy gave me a new hunger for life that will never leave me. Besides, my brother's illness taught me that I was right to have believed the impossible can happen. But I also learned that belief must be tied to action: so I created Kid's Hospital Video Network.

- Lloyd's TSB plans to award me its "Humane Heart" medal for my Diego Day School work, but my true joy comes when I hear the children shout "Hello, Masao!" every Saturday morning.

- By speaking to Nairobi professionals about society's myths about breast cancer, I learned that challenging people to see the truth about an issue can be a priceless gift. I now believe that giving others the tools to solve their problems offers much greater value to them than simply donating food, clothes, toys, or money.

Change: What You Did

- I recognized that learning how to block as well as promote angiogenesis (the development of blood vessels) would be a potentially groundbreaking strategy for developing treatments for diseases like cancer, diabetic retinopathy, and coronary heart disease. At a meeting of IdeoDNA's senior scientists and managers, I therefore initiated a debate about the company's pursuit of pure science versus the development of marketable products. I maintained that to ensure its survival, IdeoDNA had to take a more product-oriented approach and use its technology base effectively to focus on product development.

- "Internationalism via internships"—that was the unprecedented idea behind the program I enthusiastically promoted in Kagoshima, Japan, for the Global Association for Finance Student Exchange in 2005.

- To find a solution, I analyzed India's sales trends and concluded that small accounts would continue to contribute at least 50 percent of International Paper's annual business for the next 10 years. International Paper India had to nurture these accounts and serve them well to remain competitive. I recognized that our selling to these small accounts was largely limited by logistics, so I devised a new delivery method that efficiently serviced small businesses scattered throughout India.

- Last November, two friends in Israel's computer hardware industry informed me that they had developed technology that would make it possible to easily develop holographic gene chips on conventional, inexpensive DVDs. I agreed to provide the biotechnology expertise, and we quickly filed three patents for this new technology ("DNA-DVD") and developed its prototype. Six months later, together with two other cofounders, we launched Chai Laboratories and approached Toshiba and the Israeli government for venture funding.

- I saw an opportunity for Thai NYC to create symbiotic relationships: members would receive discounts for services and products offered by other members who, in turn, benefited from the increased awareness of their presence. I negotiated perks for our members with New York businesses catering to the Thai community, and I initiated a program offering reduced membership dues to members who provided discounts on their services. Seventy members agreed to offer discounts. I also partnered with two professional organizations in the New York City area that conducted excellent seminars on diverse topics of interest to the community. This strategic alliance allowed us to increase the potential scale of participation, which in turn enabled Thai NYC to organize bigger events that reduced the member cost per event.

- I could not gain Motorola Russia's support for my plan initially: management could not see the value of investing in vans just to sell to mom-and-pop stores. Instead, I needed to convince Motorola's distributors to make the investment of buying a van. To help start this process, I conducted a test in my own region, persuading my distributors to buy minivans at their own expense. This was actually a tremendously difficult undertaking since until then Motorola had traditionally paid all costs of distribution. Despite the initial negative response to my plan, I remained persistent and finally convinced my distributors to buy 12 minivans to test the program in four cities.

- Because the Drip-Rite technology was so novel, no road map existed for its implementation and application. To sell the product, I first had to develop a service offering that described how it could help clients and a methodology for implementing it. Though the Drip-Rite product had a narrow range of functionality, my experience working with sales over the previous year enabled me to show clients that it could also be used in new, unanticipated ways, from watering office plants remotely to keeping grocery stores' produce sections hydrated.

- To convince the dean that a new strategy was essential, I helped coordinate an electronic brainstorming session to which I invited former admissions officers, active alumni, former student admissions assistants, and professors who had reviewed applications for the admissions committee in the past. As the moderator, I got the group to identify the key challenges facing the graduate school's admissions process and to debate needed modifications. After the meeting, I summarized the group's observations, developed a new strategy for improving marketing reach and increasing yield, and vetted it with each of the participants. By creating an environment in which admissions challenges could be discussed in a nonthreatening and collaborative way, I was able to convince the dean to approve all six of my recommendations with minor changes.

■ It was not easy to introduce such dramatic change to so conservative an environment as a Big Four accounting firm. I was successful because I maintained open communication, had a thorough understanding of the technology, was willing to resolve conflicts, had an open attitude toward feedback, and was committed to overcoming challenge.

Change: Takeaways

■ In the end, after dedicating over 500 hours over two years to enhancing our publishing tools and processes, I conceived and executed the "better way" I had not even considered when I first joined the firm. In doing so, I progressed from a naive, conforming, and self-doubting editor to a mature, questioning, and confident manager.

■ My experience on the expandable bridge project taught me that to bring about change, I first need to understand the reasons why it is resisted. Then I need to allay the concerns of those resisting change, and, finally, I need to demonstrate the benefits change can bring. I also learned that by involving the change resistors in the process of improving the weaknesses of the change process, I can create a win-win situation that enables us to solve the problem at hand together.

- I learned several lessons about entrepreneurial leadership during this experience. First, good ideas can come from anyone, even those outside the group, so the entrepreneur must always listen. Second, the entrepreneur must be able to quickly determine which ideas are worth implementing. Third, success will often depend on the qualities and especially the dedication of the people you work with. Finally, having a common goal that benefits everyone will go a long way toward ensuring a venture's success.

- The entire experience of transforming a concept into a product taught me how to analyze business requirements and create technical specifications that address these requirements. I also learned how to negotiate with dozens of constituencies to arrive at the various agreements. I discovered that the best technical designs not only solve the problem at hand but solve them in a consensual way that wins everyone's support. But my biggest lesson was that the act of creation involves much more than creativity. As innovative as my solution was, it was the synergy between that creativity

➡

and Caterpillar's technical, marketing, and management forces that made the solution successful.

- Working for a nonprofit organization gave me my first opportunity to come up with creative ideas that benefited not only an entire organization but the larger community as well. Implementing my ideas through MetroOrganic's 60 volunteers also strengthened my leadership skills, because no one had to do what I asked them to. As a result, today I am less reticent about innovative and assertive strategies even when the risk is significant. Solving existing problems and preempting potential ones, I have learned, is possible only with a proactive, not reactive, mind.

- "Significant change" can be measured in many ways, from bottom-line impact and improved morale to compliments from executives. But, however measured, I believe that major change must be powered by the quality of the personal relationships that the change agent forms.

- The lessons I learned from the People Orbiter project sensitized me to the ways in which change and innovation can alter an organization's dynamics because they force people to fill new, unaccustomed roles. Through this and my earlier entrepreneurial experiences, I've learned the necessity of understanding the human consequences of implementing emerging technology on teams.

- I discovered that leading change means being able to deal with uncertainty, assess situations, build consensus, and achieve a shared vision by discovering solutions that draw upon everyone's talents. I also learned that to influence people to accept change, you have to understand the specific ways in which change can negatively affect people. At NuGirl Denim, I took an active interest in the designers' concerns, and although I didn't always have the right answers, I did know how to collaborate with everyone so we ultimately achieved our objectives.

- I am proud of this innovation not only because of the multimillion-dollar competitive advantage it produced for Lockheed Martin but because of the inclusive and collaborative way in whi ch I executed my plan. I employed creativity, technological understanding, perseverance, and the ability to strategically manage the uncertainty that surrounds the entry into a new government market. Despite resistance I tactfully approached the relevant people, prepared a detailed action plan based on hard data, proposed a risk-free test of my idea, and then oversaw the implementation of the new process without taking all the credit or excluding others from my success. I learned how to successfully bring about significant change that was good for the organization—even when I was the only one who initially believed in it.

Part V

Chapter 10 Perfect Phrases for Optional Essays

"If there is any important information that is relevant for your candidacy that you were unable to address elsewhere in the application, please share that information here."

(Chicago)

As Chicago Graduate School of Business's broadly worded optional topic makes clear, optional essays need not be used to explain the question marks in your application. But such "extenuating circumstance" topics are still their most common use. Uneven grades, disappointing GMAT scores, employment gaps—whatever application anomalies might cause admissions readers to jump to negative conclusions can be handily addressed in the optional essay. Less potentially damaging topics such as choice of recommenders or why you are reapplying are also suitable optional essay topics (provided the school doesn't ask you to discuss them elsewhere).

If you have no such matters to discuss, you should still consider exploiting the optional essay to present aspects of your profile not captured in the required essays—such as an unusual international experience or a leadership or community role not elsewhere described.

The perfect optional essay phrases in this chapter focus on extenuating academic-related circumstances, extenuating professional circumstances, choice of recommenders, and reapplication.

Extenuating Circumstances: GMAT and Academic

- I would like to explain to the admissions committee why my undergraduate GPA does not accurately reflect my ability to succeed in Columbia's MBA program or in my post-MBA career. In high school I was covaledictorian, an honor student, and the elected leader of three student organizations. However, during my freshman year at Loyola University I struggled to adjust to the academic rigors of the biochemistry program. A major reason was that my nontraditional high school's grading policy did not emphasize final exams, so I never learned how to prepare well for them. Moreover, as the first person in my family to attend college, I had no one I could turn to for guidance on how to balance academics and work.

- I would ask the committee to note that when I entered college, it was always my intention to be fully engaged

---

in extracurricular activities. Thus, in addition to my full course load during my four years at Bryn Mawr, I was active in three student organizations (student senate, volleyball, and student newspaper) and averaged 20 hours per week in my part-time job. Much of the time I could have spent chasing A's was devoted to fulfilling leadership responsibilities in my extracurricular commitments and working to pay for nearly half of my private university education.

- My undergraduate grades do not reflect my ability to handle the rigorous academic challenge of Harvard Business School. The primary reason is that in my last year and a half at Beloit College, my mother's health began to decline because of kidney disease, and as the only child, my father needed my help in caring for her. I took leaves of 7–10 days from Beloit College about 10 times during that period, not counting summer vacations, to travel the 575 miles to and from Thunder Bay. My grades and project work necessarily suffered. Throughout this emotionally exhausting period, my priority was my family, and my main academic objective was just to complete my degree requirements on schedule—which I did—so that I could spend time at home. This was the sole reason my academic performance fell below my Dean's List performance in my first three years.

- Because of the extensive traveling I do for Safeway (three days a week for eight months of the year), I was unable to devote sufficient time to preparing for the GMAT in a formal or sustained way. I respectfully ask the committee to take this fact into account when evaluating my score.

- While I make no excuses for my poor academic performance at Goucher, I believe the committee should understand the concrete reasons why my GPA is not indicative of my ability to succeed at Wharton. Growing up with an abusive father affected my self-esteem in ways I am still coming to grips with. Lacking any reassurance or positive role models at home, I was fearful about approaching high school teachers with even simple questions. My self-isolation prevented me from developing any mentoring relationships with adults, and hence my potential remained undiscovered. These obstacles were amplified by a childhood spent in a rural town in one of Mississippi's poorest counties. I never lacked ambition, but I had no idea what it took to succeed.

- I would like to use this essay to explain why I believe I need a second MBA. The reason is simple. My start-up experience with Dynamic Solutions in 2000 completely changed my understanding of what it takes to achieve exceptional success in the business world. When I earned my MBA at the University of Phoenix, 9/11 was just an emergency phone number, blogs were the domain of Internet geeks, the Web browser hadn't been invented, "google" was not yet a verb, and YouTube was still five years from its birth. A lot has happened to the technology world since then, and a lot has happened in my career. I now know that to build a successful business in the post–credit crunch economy I need more than a master's in engineering and an online MBA. Above all, I have learned through hard experience that having access to a network of leaders is a sine qua non for entrepreneurial success.

■ I would like to use this optional essay to explain why I believe my disappointing GMAT score does not capture the intellectual skills I'll bring to Tuck's classrooms. There has always been a disconnect between my academic performance and my performance on standardized tests, such as the SAT and GRE. On both those tests I posted average scores while I was simultaneously earning above-average grades at university. I resolved to overcome this anomaly this time, but despite enrolling in an intensive English grammar course and taking the GMAT three times, I have not been able to improve my score beyond a 670. Though I am more convinced than ever that standardized tests are not a good predictor of my success in the classroom, in business, or in life, I continue to read English intensively to improve my

➡

217

grammar skills and would be happy to take any preparatory course work you recommend before enrolling at Tuck.

- My disappointing undergraduate grades are the direct result of traumatic experiences that prevented me from focusing fully on my courses at Tulane. In May 2003, two weeks before spring finals, I was sexually assaulted by a classmate. After a brief but necessary stay in the emergency room, I spent a week in campus health services recovering. But my medical injuries, though serious, were surpassed by my emotional and psychological trauma.

Extenuating Circumstances: Damage Control

- Should my disappointing GPA raise concerns about my academic aptitude? I don't believe so. As my transcript shows, in summer 2000 I participated in a high school program that enabled me to take three UCLA courses, in which I earned a 4.0 GPA. At UCLA as a college student, I maintained a 3.42 average including demanding calculus and engineering courses in semesters when I was not distracted by duties as starting wide receiver for the Bruins football team. Moreover, up to my senior year, my transcripts show an upward trend in performance, especially as I entered my area of concentration. Finally, I have offset my poor grades in Calculus II and III by retaking them at DePaul University (earning A's in both) and completing level III of the Chartered Financial Analyst program. Finally, I've recently earned A's in an accounting and a statistics class at DePaul. I believe the full context of my academic performance demonstrates that I am more than prepared to handle the academic challenges Yale SOM offers me.

- Regarding my GMAT verbal score, today I routinely research, write, and present consulting proposals and reports externally for Advanced Informatics' clients and internally for our management and business development group. Last year I was honored to submit a white paper on informatics trends for an industry conference sponsored by AI. It was nominated for a prestigious Best Practices Award. Finally, AI would never have placed me in charge of more than 10 client-facing auditing engagements annually if they had any concerns about my verbal skills. I am confident in my ability to write and speak English like a native and believe that the evidence should inspire this same confidence in the admissions committee.

- It has been more than eight years since I graduated from university. As my résumé amply demonstrates, I have matured both professionally and personally. My success in a complex and rigorous profession, not grades in courses I took a decade ago, should constitute the primary desideratum in determining my potential for academic success at Stanford. I have demonstrated a consistent record of achievement and communicative skill that should greatly minimize the significance of my undergraduate transcript.

Extenuating Circumstances: Professional

■ I would like to explain in this essay why there is a three-month gap in my work history, from January 2006 to April 2006. When San Diego's residential real estate market began to implode, mortgage services companies like Pacific Escrow were the first to bear the brunt. Shortly after Christmas 2005, I was notified that my escrow support group was being eliminated, despite our award-winning work during the preceding three years. I was devastated, but I immediately began seeking a new position. Unfortunately, the Southern California housing market continued to worsen, and I was unable to find a job until April, when I joined Balboa Debt Collection Services as a compliance manager. Throughout my three months of full-time job searching, I continued to volunteer weekly as an English tutor at my church, began and completed a finance course at Poway Community College, and helped my husband open a new surfing supplies shop in suburban San Diego. I believe the reasons for my brief unemployment and the activities I pursued during it reflect positively on me and my potential for success at UC Irvine.

- A minuscule fraction of all medical school students—less than 1 percent—do not graduate. Most who leave do so, like me, for deeply personal reasons and no doubt find their decision to be one of the hardest they have ever faced. I would like to devote this optional essay to explaining my reason for leaving medical school. What kind of life would I be leading if every patient's death or incurable diagnosis left me with a feeling of failure and despair? So I could find my answer to that question, I was granted a one-year leave from medical school at the end of my second year.

- I would like to explain more fully why I decided to leave Mercury Consultants to join 1–2–3-Go Technologies. My three and a half years at Mercury were a valuable learning experience for me, but by early 2007 I had reached the point where the learning and challenge were beginning to decelerate. Moreover, stepping back, I recognized that my consulting job was not as rewarding as I wanted because I rarely got the chance to implement my ideas across the full life cycle of an engagement. Just as important, I had learned that the engagements I most enjoyed were for high-tech clients like RazorsEdge, NeonThrust Group, and, above all, 1–2–3-Go.

Choice of Recommenders

- I have not asked my current supervisor at Sunoco to submit a recommendation on my behalf because I have been with the firm for only three months. My supervisor is quite pleased with my work, but my projects have not advanced sufficiently for him to comment meaningfully on my performance. Moreover, my supervisors at Marathon Oil and Cascade Aeronautics worked with me closely on multiple projects extending over my two years with each firm. Thus they are in a much better position to comment authoritatively on my performance and potential. Second, I wanted to choose recommenders who would show the Cornell admissions committee my ability to perform successfully in varied industries. By selecting one recommender from a major domestic oil corporation and the other from a small international aviation technology firm, I hope the admissions committee will gain a better, more broadly based appreciation of the professional skills and interpersonal qualities I want to bring to the Johnson School.

- I did not ask my current supervisor at Alpine MicroBrewery for a recommendation because past experience tells me he would not view my pursuit of an MBA favorably, however positively he regards me professionally. If he knew I was contemplating leaving the firm, it would adversely affect my short-term ability to gain challenging assignments and my long-term prospects in the company. Moreover, I have supplied one additional recommendation from Dr. Watanabe, my supervisor at Sudami Chemicals, who worked with me extensively for more than 16 months.

Reapplication

■ In the 12 months since my first application to Indiana's Kelley School, I have made significant changes in my life, which make me a stronger applicant for admission. First, though I was on track for promotion at CapGemini, after successfully concluding a four-person, $500,000 project for Saskatchewan Financial Services, I decided to leave CapGemini last January for a career opportunity closer to my health-care goals (described in my goal statement last year). Working for 10 months as a corporate development manager at Iredexsys Therapeutics has given me more responsibility and bottom-line impact than any other position in my career. Today I can offer my Kelley classmates insights into two industries and the leadership experiences of a manager whose five-person team has won two internal awards. In addition to this exciting career transition, I have made a substantial change in my community life. This summer, I became a mentor for a troubled Hispanic teen named Arturo through Houston Big Brothers/Big Sisters. My goal in this one-year commitment has been to help Arturo apply to, be accepted for, and enroll in college. I have already convinced him to apply to college (no easy thing), and I am now working hard to guide him through the demanding process of selecting and applying to the programs that will benefit him most. Helping Arturo has been one of the most challenging and gratifying experiences of my life, and I am looking forward to sharing my mentorship experiences with my Kelley class.

- My goal since my first application to Yale SOM has not been to throw out my original career goals or try to replace the strengths I stated in my last application with entirely new ones. Rather than reinvent the wheel, I have instead spent the past two years defining my goals more sharply and building on my existing leadership and entrepreneurship skills. Though entrepreneurship is still my long-term goal, my intensive experiences in private equity since 2006 have enabled me to see the legal, operational, financial, and recruiting complexities behind successfully launched start-ups. I have also been able to identify more specific segments of the economy where my future consumer finance firm can gain profitable traction.

- Reapplying to Michigan is not a decision I take lightly. This past spring, I was accepted at two excellent MBA programs. I made the difficult decision to turn down their offers and reapply to Ross School, both for personal reasons and because I continue to believe that Michigan's MBA program is the best one for me. One reason I decided to postpone business school until fall 2009 is the failing health of my father, whose diabetes worsened this past spring and led to his temporary hospitalization. Because neither of my brothers was in a position to help support my immigrant parents through my father's medical crisis, I delayed school and lent both my financial and emotional resources to my family.

Chapter 11 Perfect Phrases for Business School Interviews

Some business schools try to interview all their applicants; some interview only those who've survived an initial screening review. And other schools' interview policies fall somewhere in between. Whatever the policy of the schools you're applying to, the business school interview will be an important stage in your MBA admissions hunt. Whether you interview with admissions staff, alumni, students, or even faculty, a lousy interview performance can sink your chances, and a brilliant one can advance them.

We've seen that most B-school essay questions can be categorized within eight basic topics. The range of possible interview questions is no doubt vaster. After all, where most business schools limit themselves to four to seven essays, even the standard 30-minute interview can cover 10 or more questions, ranging from why you majored in physical education to which kind of vegetable you would be (and why) to what you think of the Chicago Bears.

The impossibility of predicting the interview questions is partly why business schools continue to conduct them: they test you in ways essays do not. Nevertheless, there are several interview questions that you can be fairly confident will be asked in some form. We provide perfect phrases for these core questions in this chapter. These core topics are followed by perfect phrases for three broad categories of questions that you should also practice for: behavioral questions (in which the interviewer asks hypothetical or situational questions to see how you act in certain circumstances), tough questions ("Tell me about yourself"), and questions you should be ready to ask the interviewer when your interrogation is over.

The Core Questions

"What are your career goals?"

■ My short-term career plan after Virginia is to work for a couple of years at a venture capital firm like Bain Capital or Silver Lake Partners. Evaluating alternative energy firms for possible funding, I'll have a great opportunity to recognize emerging technologies, develop my venture analysis and mentoring skills, refine my own business plan, and establish contacts in the energy and VC industry. My long-term career goal is to launch an alternative energy firm that will focus on sustainable but also scalable alternative energy solutions such as wind-powered desalination plants or non-silicon-based solar power farms. With a Darden MBA I'll be ideally positioned to ensure that my firm attracts enough seed money, recruits top scientific talent, and aligns itself with a major energy company that can help us leverage our technological breakthroughs. I'm really excited about the opportunities that are emerging.

- My short-term post-MBA goal is to work as an investment research analyst covering emerging markets either for an investment bank with a presence in Southeast Asia, such as Lehman Brothers, or at a mutual fund specializing in the region, such as Matthews International's Pacific Tiger Fund. Combined with the special insights I have gained through my knowledge of China and Vietnam—both their cultures and their economies—this career phase will give me a rich and nuanced foundation in the market and its companies. In the long term, I plan to exploit my investment research experience through a position as a fund manager. Based in the United States, Singapore, or Shanghai, I will run a Southeast Asia emerging markets fund that enables me to travel frequently to the region to visit companies and speak to company managers. Eventually—say, 10 to 15 years out—I hope to start my own fund focused on Southeast Asia or maybe even entirely on Vietnam, which I expect to grow as quickly as China did during its initial breakout period.

"Why do you want an MBA?"

- The skills I've gained in project management and finance at General Foods have given me a great foundation for my post-MBA marketing career. But technology management-to-marketing is a big career switch, and I need the MBA to help me fill in my specific knowledge gaps, for example, the principles of advertising, how to interpret statistical data from market research, how to price products, strategic marketing planning—even the use of branding partnerships with other companies. The MBA is the best way to quickly but also thoroughly ramp up my knowledge of these areas. Of course, an MBA program will also enhance my "soft" leadership skills, sharpen my quantitative and analytical skills, enable me to network with sharp, talented people from different backgrounds, and experience a summer internship that will open a door for me to transition into marketing.

"Why now?"

- Well, it's really only been in the past one or two years that I've known for sure that private equity is the path I want to devote my career to. Blackstone's acquisition of my firm forced me to learn in a hurry what private equity firms do and what kinds of impacts they have. When I began to see the positive effects they were having on Remington's operations and strategy, I sought out some of Blackstone's contact people for our firm and learned a lot more. That led to informational interviews with managers at Apollo Management and Bain Capital. I just became really passionate about PE at that point, and I knew it was what I should be doing. Needless to say, with my background in engineering there's no way to break into private equity unless I "retool" with an MBA. And at 27, it doesn't make sense to wait.

"Why our school?"

■ I first learned of MIT Sloan before I was even seriously considering an MBA. Mary Goffin, a Sloan MBA at my firm, was and is very active as an alumna, and she was always singing the praises of MIT's MBA program. When I became serious about the MBA, I remembered what she had said about Sloan's superlative technology resources, including the Center for Information Systems Research, Productivity from Information Technology, and Center for e-Business. I began exploring the program on my own, including a campus visit last spring, and was impressed by the students I spoke with, including Tim Zhang, Beatrice Ellfeldt, and Vijay Singh. I loved the idea of the "First-year Challenge," the emphasis on experiential learning through the leadership courses, and the unique Sloan Innovation Period. Since entrepreneurship is my goal, the $1K Warm-Up Business Idea Competition and the MIT $50K Entrepreneurship Competition will be fantastic opportunities for me. I'd be happy to go into more detail about the Sloan classes, professors, and student clubs that I'm excited about.

Résumé-Keyed Core Questions

"Walk me through your résumé."

- I majored in biochemistry in college because I planned on becoming a doctor. A summer job as an equipment tester at my father's pharmaceuticals firm and a macroeconomics course sparked my interest in business. So after eye-opening internships at E*Trade and Mercer Consulting, I accepted an offer to become an associate consultant in the Chicago office of McKinsey & Company. McKinsey's hypothesis-driven approach to problem-solving fit my science background perfectly. I also wanted a general introduction to finance, marketing, strategy, or operations in a variety of industries, which consulting for McKinsey could give me. A McKinsey project gave me my first taste of entrepreneurship. My colleague and I created from the ground up the business plan for a client's technology start-up, working directly with their CEO and dozens of client staff. Our plan was accepted and implemented, and it ultimately led to a business that today generates $100 million in revenue. This project sparked my interest in entrepreneurship, so after three years at McKinsey I moved to Warburg Pincus to get insight into new ventures from the operational and investment side. My year at Warburg has really broadened the way I think about companies. I have developed an in-depth knowledge of finance and have been able to work with companies' balance sheets much more than I would have at McKinsey. After three years in consulting and one in private equity, I'm ready to get the skills to become a successful entrepreneur.

"Why did you leave JeoVision after only six months?"

- That was a difficult experience for me, but one I take full responsibility for. I had been working there as an IT contractor for about six months in the sales and marketing department. Because I was looking for ways to break into technical sales, I loved the environment and the department. My client manager knew of my interest and went out of his way to expose me to some of the sales functions. When a full-time opening came up for a technical liaison with the development department, the sales and marketing client manager suggested that I take it and promised me it was really a stepping-stone position into a direct technical sales position. That would have been just what I wanted, but it didn't turn out to be the case. In fact, the full-time position took me even further from JeoVision's sales and marketing functions, and turned out to be a straight technical role. I should have done more due diligence rather than rely on the client manager's assurances. Anyway, when Oracle offered me a true technical sales position—exactly what I had been looking for—I decided to jump at the chance. I learned a lot about doing my "homework" and taking responsibility for my actions from that experience.

"Could you explain this gap of six months on your résumé in 2008?"

- Sure. As you know, the subprime crisis led to Bear Stearns's purchase for pennies by Morgan Stanley, and in April, my entire department was downsized—15 people in all, regardless of experience, seniority, education. As the credit markets were still reeling, most of the companies I would have looked to for work were not hiring. I interviewed at over 20 firms in the space of six months, networked at at least 10 industry events and conferences, and used my personal network to do informational interviews outside the industry. But the economy wasn't be friendly to job hunters. Fortunately, I also used my time between jobs to deepen my involvement at The Hope Place, mentoring two kids, who are now my good buddies. I also completed my CFA III exam, studied for the GMAT, and began visiting business schools, including Anderson. It was a challenging period for me, but I never gave up, and finally this May, Banco Popular offered me an interesting position in its merchant services group. Since this aligned with my post-MBA international goals, I decided to take it and apply for your Fully Employed MBA program.

Behavioral Questions

"If you were working on a project with a team of peers late at night and they had an opinion entirely different from yours, how would you manage the situation so that the team completed the assignment the next day?"

■ In these kinds of situations, I first ask a lot of questions so I can clearly understand each person's point of view. If the explanations they give me persuade me that my position is flawed, I back off my position as appropriate and offer a new solution that integrates their position and the elements of mine that I still believe in. We can then proceed forward. If their answers to my questions fail to convince me that my approach needs revising, I need to consider how important it is to me that our project's success take priority over my team's unity. I mean, I might be willing to accept a less-than-optimal solution for this project because I don't feel I have time to convince my teammates or I believe there will be long-term negative impact on the team's cohesiveness if I try to push my position on this project too hard. It would depend very much on the context. But if I believe so strongly in my position—for example, if I believe my teammates' solution could have extremely negative consequences—I will use all my persuasive and analytical powers to make the best possible case for my solution, specifically identifying the reasons why I believe their positions are flawed. Wherever possible, I will offer compromises so they won't feel "defeated" or resent my resistance. For example, I might offer to support their position on some other project if they buy into mine on this one. Or I might try to incorporate aspects of their position that won't be harmful to the net outcome if they agree to follow my position on the really mission-critical aspects of the project. If I am certain my position is the best solution for the project, I have enough confidence in my negotiation and interpersonal skills to believe that I could eventually persuade them. I have encountered some examples of this kind of situation from my professional life if you'd like to hear them.

"What kind of manager are you? How do you motivate people? What is your managerial style?"

- I consider myself to be an inclusive, collaborative manager with high standards but a nonconfrontational style. I developed this leadership philosophy as class president at McMaster University and refined it at as a corporate manager for ZNG Systems in the United

States and Lenovo in China. It's based on three basic principles: taking initiative and motivating team members through encouragement, synergizing skills, trust, and shared vision; welcoming criticism as feedback toward improving the process; and solving problems through rigorous analysis and hard data. When I first joined ZNG in 2002, for example, the company had just been dealt a major blow when the virtualization industry standards group omitted its core technology from the industry standard. When ZNG's stock nosedived, management called a meeting, but because we had just enjoyed a successful round of venture funding, no one really sensed the urgency. Though I was only a junior manager I stood up and made what I meant to be an inspiring speech on behalf of focusing less on our promising but still-incubating products and putting greater energy into reducing the time-to-market for our more fully developed products. I was surprised by how much flak I received for that, but I didn't let it rattle me. I asked for time to put together a detailed proposal and timeline for repurposing our product development efforts. I also explicitly asked my critics to review my proposal and offer their feedback. This won over management and some of my critics, and two weeks later I presented a proposal, which had definitely been rigorously worked over and improved by my critics. Because that proposal was thoroughly backed up by data from our product development staff, competitor intelligence, and a couple of germane case studies, it won the day, and today I'm working directly with the CTO and the entire product development staff in implementing my new time-to-market plan. I'll bring this same leadership style to my Tuck study group.

Tough Questions

"Tell me about yourself."

- Sure. Though I was born and raised in middle-class Peoria, Illinois, I think I can say I've led a pretty unusual life. When I was 10, my father took a sabbatical from his teaching job and bought a sailboat, which he and my mother, sister, and I sailed around the Caribbean for two years. The exposure to the cultural variety of this region was an incredible revelation for me, and ever since then I have been a travel and language nut. So far I've lived or worked in four countries, including Norway, Panama, and the U.K., and I speak three languages fluently: English, Norwegian, and German. I think I can offer a lot in terms of cross-cultural insights to my Yale classmates. When I was 16, my family moved to Oslo, Norway, which was a bit difficult for me at first because of the cold winters and language barrier. I worked hard at learning the language though, and eventually made friends who showed me Scandinavia's hot spots and backpacked with me through Europe and Russia.

My technology knowledge grew directly from my desire to be an "international person." I joined Germany's SAP right after graduating from Humboldt Universität. SAP was an exciting place. I worked on SAP's business process outsourcing efforts, and in my spare time I started a successful travel-rating Web site similar to TripAdvisor but Europe-focused. This entrepreneurial experience gave me an interest in product marketing, which I pursued by joining the start-up Crescat Group, a global technology consultancy. Within a year, I was promoted to director of development, in charge of all of our business development activities for the firm's Western Europe region. Leading teams as large as 15, I played a key role in growing Crescat's top-line revenue by 350 percent.

My success gave me the resources to start SeaGuide, a travel-based youth leadership program similar to Outward Bound but more nautically based. That's grown by leaps and bounds. We now have chapters in nine countries. To get social entrepreneurship skills to professionalize and expand SeaGuide is why I'm seeking the MBA. I'm confident my cross-cultural, technology management, and social entrepreneurship skills will enable me to add a lot to my Tepper class.

"Why should we accept you? What would you add to the program?"

■ Well, I think I can bring a pretty diverse perspective to my classmates that will really enhance their experience. Professionally, I have unusual leadership exposure to both the public and private sectors. As the commander of gunnery crews on two Singaporean navy frigates, for example, I was exposed to the military's unusual technical and organizational demands at sea. But I was also later assigned to develop a system for motivating and tracking the performance of naval recruits and to command a naval facility on the Malaysian border. As a technical manager at Flextronics I have learned how to quickly build teams to manage the complexity, competition, and change of the outsourced electronics manufacturing industry.

Personally, I can offer the insights of someone who led effectively in Singapore's armed forces, a melting pot of Malays, Chinese, Indians, and Eurasians. As both a Singaporean and ethnic German, by any definition I would be considered a "diversity" applicant. But as an avid scuba diver I also bring my unique vision of the global community. Scuba diving opens up an entire "global community" of life that most people never experience. I have found that diving with people from every walk of life always creates bridges across cultural and language differences as we appreciate and explore the diversity of the underwater world that binds everyone on earth. My family's story and my involvement in the Pacific Rim Environment Fund add to the diverse contribution I can bring to Stanford, and I'd be glad to talk about them.

"What is the primary weakness in your application?"

■ Probably the fact that early on my career basically centered on research, so I didn't gain any leadership opportunities for three or more years. However, I began to address this two years ago when I pursued and won a lab manager position at Fusion BioEnergy and then helped start GreenFuel. I think I proved my managerial potential by leading the efficiency changes in this group during the integration of Fusion and British Petroleum. Moreover, in the process of launching GreenFuel, I was able to set a vision for the company, begin to implement that vision, and achieve tangible results. When you look at my management successes of the past few years—all achieved with only my technical degree and my own leadership instincts—I think I have demonstrated strong leadership potential.

Questions for the Interviewer

For the Admissions Committee

- "Is the new dean planning any major changes that will affect next year's entering class?"
- "What are the opportunities for students to get involved in or help out in the admissions process?"
- "I read that Dean Chen wants to expand your offerings in the human resources specialization. What changes are likely within the next year or so?"

For Students

- "Have you taken any courses with Professor Jenarczak or Thirumalai? What are they like as teachers?"
- "Which student clubs are most popular in your class?"
- "Do most first-years live on campus?"
- "What's the best place off-campus to socialize?"
- "What has surprised you most about Chicago since becoming a student?"

For Alumni

- "How has an INSEAD MBA helped you in your own career?"
- "What aspects of your MBA experience have been most useful to you in your post-MBA career?"
- "How helpful has the school's network been to you since you graduated?"
- "What are the opportunities for alumni to stay connected or involved with the school? Is the chapter here in San Jose pretty active?"

Closing Thoughts

There are no magic bullets for business school admission. At the end of the day, what you (and others) write and say about you in your application will play a huge role in your odds of success. And the words that succeed are usually the ones that are backed up with the most honesty, self-knowledge, and effort. Remember this as you consult this and other admissions guidebooks. Admissions officers read books like these too, and they have an uncanny ability (honed on the job) to recall passages they've encountered before. More importantly, they have an uncanny ability to detect when an applicant's essay rings false. For these reasons alone, do yourself a favor and use this book's ready-to-use phrases only as models to study, inspirations to emulate, or even first-draft crutches on the way to your own voice. In the end, the only "perfect" phrase is your own.

About the Author

Paul Bodine is the author of *Great Application Essays for Business School, Great Personal Statements for Law School, Perfect Phrases for Law School Acceptance*, and *Perfect Phrases for Medical School Acceptance*. One of America's most experienced admissions consultants (serving clients since 1997), his clients have earned admission to such elite business schools as Harvard, Stanford, the University of Pennsylvania (Wharton), MIT (Sloan), Northwestern (Kellogg), the University of Chicago, Columbia, Dartmouth (Tuck), Berkeley (Haas), the University of Michigan, London Business School, INSEAD, New York University, UCLA (Anderson), Duke, Virginia (Darden), and Yale. A graduate of the University of Chicago and Johns Hopkins University, he lives in Southern California.